1st EDITION

Perspectives on Modern World History

The Arab-Israeli Six-Day War

1st EDITION

Perspectives on Modern World History

The Arab-Israeli Six-Day War

Jeff Hay

Editor

GREENHAVEN PRESS

A part of Gale, Cengage Learning

Detroit • New York • San Francisco • New Haven, Conn • Waterville, Maine • London

Elizabeth Des Chenes, *Director, Publishing Solutions*

For more information, contact:
Greenhaven Press
27500 Drake Rd.
Farmington Hills, MI 48331-3535
Or you can visit our Internet site at gale.cengage.com.

LIBRARY OF CONGRESS CATALOGING-IN-PUBLICATION DATA

The Arab-Israeli six-day war / Jeff Hay, book editor.
p. cm. -- (Perspectives on modern world history)
Includes bibliographical references and index.
ISBN 978-0-7377-6361-4 (hardcover)
1. Israel-Arab War, 1967. 2. Israel-Arab War, 1967--Sources. I. Hay, Jeff.
DS127.A7745 2012
956.04'6--dc23 2012022606

Printed in the United States of America
1 2 3 4 5 6 7 16 15 14 13 12

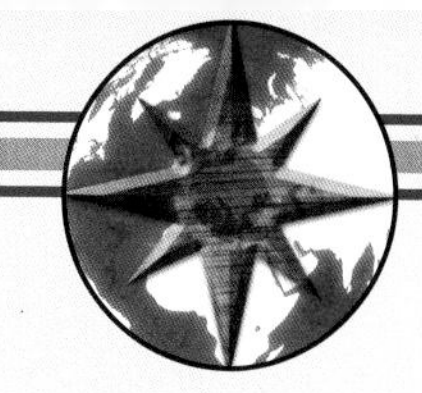

CONTENTS

CHAPTER 2 Controversies and Perspectives on the Arab-Israeli Six-Day War

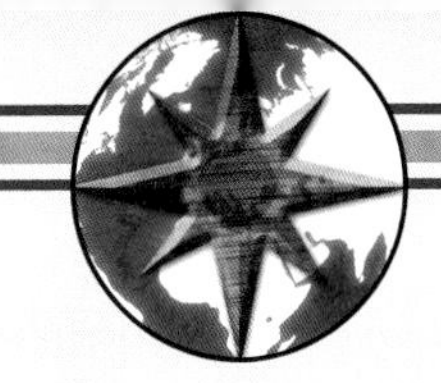

FOREWORD

> *"History cannot give us a program for the future, but it can give us a fuller understanding of ourselves, and of our common humanity, so that we can better face the future."*
>
> *—Robert Penn Warren, American poet and novelist*

The history of each nation is punctuated by momentous events that represent turning points for that nation, with an impact felt far beyond its borders. These events—displaying the full range of human capabilities, from violence, greed, and ignorance to heroism, courage, and strength—are nearly always complicated and multifaceted. Any student of history faces the challenge of grasping the many strands that constitute such world-changing events as wars, social movements, and environmental disasters. But understanding these significant historic events can be enhanced by exposure to a variety of perspectives, whether of people involved intimately or of ones observing from a distance of miles or years. Understanding can also be increased by learning about the controversies surrounding such events and exploring hot-button issues from multiple angles. Finally, true understanding of important historic events involves knowledge of the events' human impact—of the ways such events affected people in their everyday lives—all over the world.

Perspectives on Modern World History examines global historic events from the twentieth century onward by presenting analysis and observation from numerous vantage points. Each volume offers high school, early college level, and general interest readers a thematically arranged anthology of previously published materials that address a major historical event, with an emphasis on international coverage. Each volume opens with background information on the event, then presents the controversies surrounding that event, and concludes with first-person narratives from people who lived through the event or were affected by it. By providing primary sources from the time of the event, as well as relevant commentary surrounding the event, this series can be used to inform debate, help develop critical thinking skills, increase global awareness, and enhance an understanding of international perspectives on history.

Material in each volume is selected from a diverse range of sources, including journals, magazines, newspapers, nonfiction books, personal narratives, speeches, congressional testimony, government documents, pamphlets, organization newsletters, and position papers. Articles taken from these sources are carefully edited and introduced to provide context and background. Each volume of Perspectives on Modern World History includes an array of views on events of global significance. Much of the material comes from international sources and from US sources that provide extensive international coverage.

Each volume in the Perspectives on Modern World History series also includes:

- A full-color **world map**, offering context and geographic perspective.
- An annotated **table of contents** that provides a brief summary of each essay in the volume.
- An **introduction** specific to the volume topic.
- For each viewpoint, a brief **introduction** that has notes about the author and source of the viewpoint, and that provides a summary of its main points.
- Full-color **charts**, **graphs**, **maps**, and other visual representations.

- Informational **sidebars** that explore the lives of key individuals, give background on historical events, or explain scientific or technical concepts.
- A **glossary** that defines key terms, as needed.
- A **chronology** of important dates preceding, during, and immediately following the event.
- A **bibliography** of additional books, periodicals, and websites for further research.
- A comprehensive **subject index** that offers access to people, places, and events cited in the text.

Perspectives on Modern World History is designed for a broad spectrum of readers who want to learn more about not only history but also current events, political science, government, international relations, and sociology—students doing research for class assignments or debates, teachers and faculty seeking to supplement course materials, and others wanting to improve their understanding of history. Each volume of Perspectives on Modern World History is designed to illuminate a complicated event, to spark debate, and to show the human perspective behind the world's most significant happenings of recent decades.

INTRODUCTION

In May 2011, US president Barack Obama proposed that Israel return to the borders it possessed before the Arab-Israeli Six-Day War of 1967, suggesting that such a return, with some modifications, might pave the way for the creation of an independent Palestinian state. This might help provide a lasting solution to one of the most intractable geopolitical conflicts in modern history: Arab resentment over the status of Palestinian refugees. Although some Palestinians cling to the belief that the properties they lost to Israel should be returned to them, and others envision a single, larger Israel in which Palestinians and Israeli Jews will live as equals, the idea of a "two-state solution" remains predominant. By making his comments on this two-state solution, Obama reminded listeners that the legacies of the Six-Day War remain very much alive in the twenty-first century.

The Six-Day War resulted in a massive and unexpected victory for Israel over a coalition of Arab states that included Egypt, Syria, and Jordan, as well as smaller forces from Iraq. Thanks to its successes on the battlefield, the small nation of Israel, only ten miles wide at its narrowest point, was able to expand its territory by three times. It took possession of the Sinai Peninsula, the Gaza Strip, the Golan Heights, and the West Bank (also known as the Jordan River Valley). In addition, Israeli forces moved into the Arab neighborhoods of East Jerusalem, thereby taking possession of areas containing sites most holy to Jews, including the Western Wall, a remnant of an ancient Jewish temple destroyed thousands of years ago by the Romans. This situation has created a lasting problem because the area contains sites holy to Muslims and Christians as well. Some Palestinian activists refuse to consider the possibility of a Palestinian state without East Jerusalem as its capital, while Israel will likely never give it up.

The 1967 war had other legacies as well. It showed that Israel was now a major Middle Eastern power that could not be easily "pushed into the sea," as some Arab leaders had hoped. Israel's successes, moreover, attracted foreign investment, greater support from Western nations such as the United States, and new waves of Jewish immigrants to the country. Meanwhile, the influence of Egyptian president Gamal Abdel Nasser, a prominent figure in the Arab world, waned rapidly. Finally, the war turned hundreds of thousands of Palestinian Arabs into refugees or second-class citizens—as many of them termed it—in the Israeli state. The Palestine Liberation Organization (PLO), formed in 1964, soon grew more influential as a voice for the more radical of these refugees.

In the first months of 1967, few would have thought such drastic changes were possible. Israel was a small, poor nation that had little support from the outside world. It was also a very new country, having been founded only in 1948. Arab powers such as Egypt and Syria, by contrast, had large armies and aid from the Soviet Union, one of the world's superpowers. These Arab powers also had long-standing resentments toward Israel because of the status of Palestinian Arab refugees as a result of the creation of Israel. A recent past of military confrontations added to the tensions. Israel defeated an Arab coalition in 1948 while, in 1956, Nasser enjoyed a partial victory when his effort to nationalize the Suez Canal succeeded in the face of Israeli, British, and French opposition.

Attacks by militants and terrorists, a frequent problem in border areas, increased in the first part of 1967, putting Israel on edge. Meanwhile both the Egyptians and the Syrians began stepping up their anti-Israel rhetoric, stating once again their readiness to try to "push Israel into the sea." Tensions mounted rapidly when, in response to a false report from the Soviet Union that Israel was going to launch an attack on Syria, the Egyptians began a massive military buildup in the border areas of the Sinai Peninsula. Nasser also demanded the removal of a United Nations peacekeeping force, which had been in place in the Sinai Peninsula since 1957 and closed off Israel's access to the Suez Canal and Red Sea.

Despite Nasser's dramatic speeches, it was Israel that fired the first shots. On June 5, Israeli pilots destroyed much of the Egyptian Air Force on the ground, while soon after their ground forces bottled up Egypt's forces in the Sinai. Egypt accepted a ceasefire on June 8. Jordan, which sent its forces into the West Bank and launched shells on the Israeli city Tel Aviv, withdrew its armies on June 7. Syria, fighting primarily in the area of the Golan Heights, entered into a ceasefire on June 10 that was partially brokered by the United Nations.

In the months that followed, Israel signaled its willingness to return the Sinai to Egypt and the Golan Heights to Syria provided satisfactory peace treaties could be reached. They were not. Instead, Arab leaders meeting in Khartoum, Sudan, resolved to stick to the "3 no's": no to peace with Israel, no to diplomatic recognition of Israel, and no to negotiation with Israel. The United Nations continued to pay great attention to the problem, passing Resolution 242 in November 1967, which demanded that Israel return the territories it had occupied and that the various parties prepare for continued talks.

Some of the territorial and diplomatic issues resulting from the Six-Day War have been addressed in the years since 1967. In 1978, Egypt agreed to grant Israel official diplomatic recognition in the Camp David Accords, while Israel agreed to return Sinai to Egyptian possession. Then, following the Oslo Accords of 1993, the Palestinians gained self-rule over the Gaza Strip and the city of Jericho in the West Bank. Palestinian leaders abandoned their extremist rhetoric and officially recognized Israel's right to exist. The nation of Jordan has also established full diplomatic relations with Israel, although Syria has yet to do so.

Other issues remain sources of tension. Before 1993, the PLO, the closest thing Palestinians had to a leadership organization, was often associated with terrorist attacks against Israel, especially during the 1970s. It is also connected with the first "intifada," a wave of strikes, demonstrations, boycotts, and periodic violence that lasted from 1987 to 1992. A second intifada followed from 2000 to 2005, after the Palestinian Authority replaced the PLO in the mid-1990s. Even with its ties to terrorist organizations such as Hezbollah and Hamas, the Palestinian Authority has emerged as a legitimate governing body. As such, it is generally thought to have more negotiating authority than the PLO, which was more closely associated with terrorism and other non-state acts as opposed to governmental functions like providing power and water, policing, and engaging in diplomatic relations.

The Israelis have established Jewish settlements in the West Bank, further cementing the region as Israeli territory. The construction of these controversial settlements continues. They also claim that they are treating Palestinians within their borders well, a claim many Palestinians reject, noting that there is still no separate Palestinian state nor, as of early 2012, any attempt to negotiate one.

While Israel has been willing to give back a great deal of the territory it gained in the Six-Day War, there are some lands it does not want to give up. The West Bank in particular is seen as necessary to Israel's national security as it provides the nation with a defensible border to its east. Not all experts, even Israeli ones, agree, arguing that the nature of twenty-first-century warfare does not require borders to be defended by large land armies. Meanwhile, Israel maintains control of Jerusalem, although Islamic holy sites remain under the administration of neighboring Jordan.

In his 2011 speech, President Obama suggested that "land swaps" might provide a solution. This would require Israel and the Palestinian Authority, probably with some form of international involvement, to exchange various territories. Such swaps, Obama and other advocates suggest, would allow for the creation of a Palestinian state and, at the same time, allow Israel to remain militarily secure. Whether or not land swaps are truly possible, Obama's suggestions are reminders that many of the issues introduced by the Arab-Israeli Six-Day War remain extremely complicated and unresolved. *Perspectives on Modern World History: The Arab-Israeli Six-Day War* examines the events preceding and following the war and their impact on the world today.

World Map

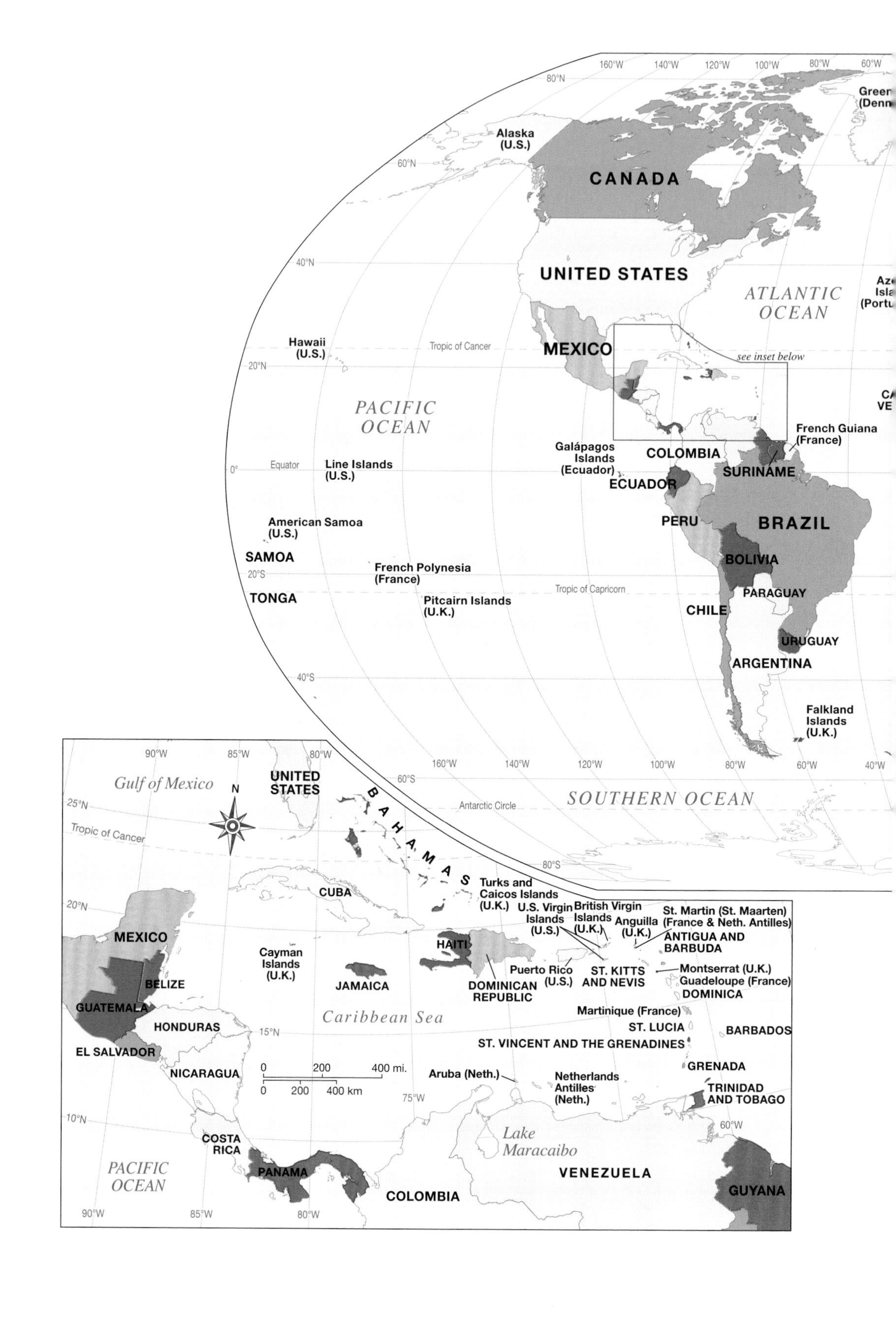

CANADA
Alaska (U.S.)
UNITED STATES
ATLANTIC OCEAN
MEXICO
see inset below
Hawaii (U.S.)
Tropic of Cancer
PACIFIC OCEAN
French Guiana (France)
Galápagos Islands (Ecuador)
COLOMBIA
SURINAME
Equator
Line Islands (U.S.)
ECUADOR
PERU
BRAZIL
American Samoa (U.S.)
SAMOA
BOLIVIA
French Polynesia (France)
TONGA
Tropic of Capricorn
PARAGUAY
Pitcairn Islands (U.K.)
CHILE
URUGUAY
ARGENTINA
Falkland Islands (U.K.)
SOUTHERN OCEAN
Antarctic Circle
Gulf of Mexico
BAHAMAS
Turks and Caicos Islands (U.K.)
CUBA
U.S. Virgin Islands (U.S.)
British Virgin Islands (U.K.)
Anguilla (U.K.)
St. Martin (St. Maarten) (France & Neth. Antilles)
ANTIGUA AND BARBUDA
HAITI
Cayman Islands (U.K.)
JAMAICA
DOMINICAN REPUBLIC
Puerto Rico (U.S.)
ST. KITTS AND NEVIS
Montserrat (U.K.)
Guadeloupe (France)
DOMINICA
BELIZE
GUATEMALA
HONDURAS
Caribbean Sea
Martinique (France)
ST. LUCIA
BARBADOS
EL SALVADOR
ST. VINCENT AND THE GRENADINES
GRENADA
NICARAGUA
Aruba (Neth.)
Netherlands Antilles (Neth.)
TRINIDAD AND TOBAGO
0 200 400 mi.
0 200 400 km
COSTA RICA
Lake Maracaibo
PANAMA
VENEZUELA
COLOMBIA
GUYANA
PACIFIC OCEAN

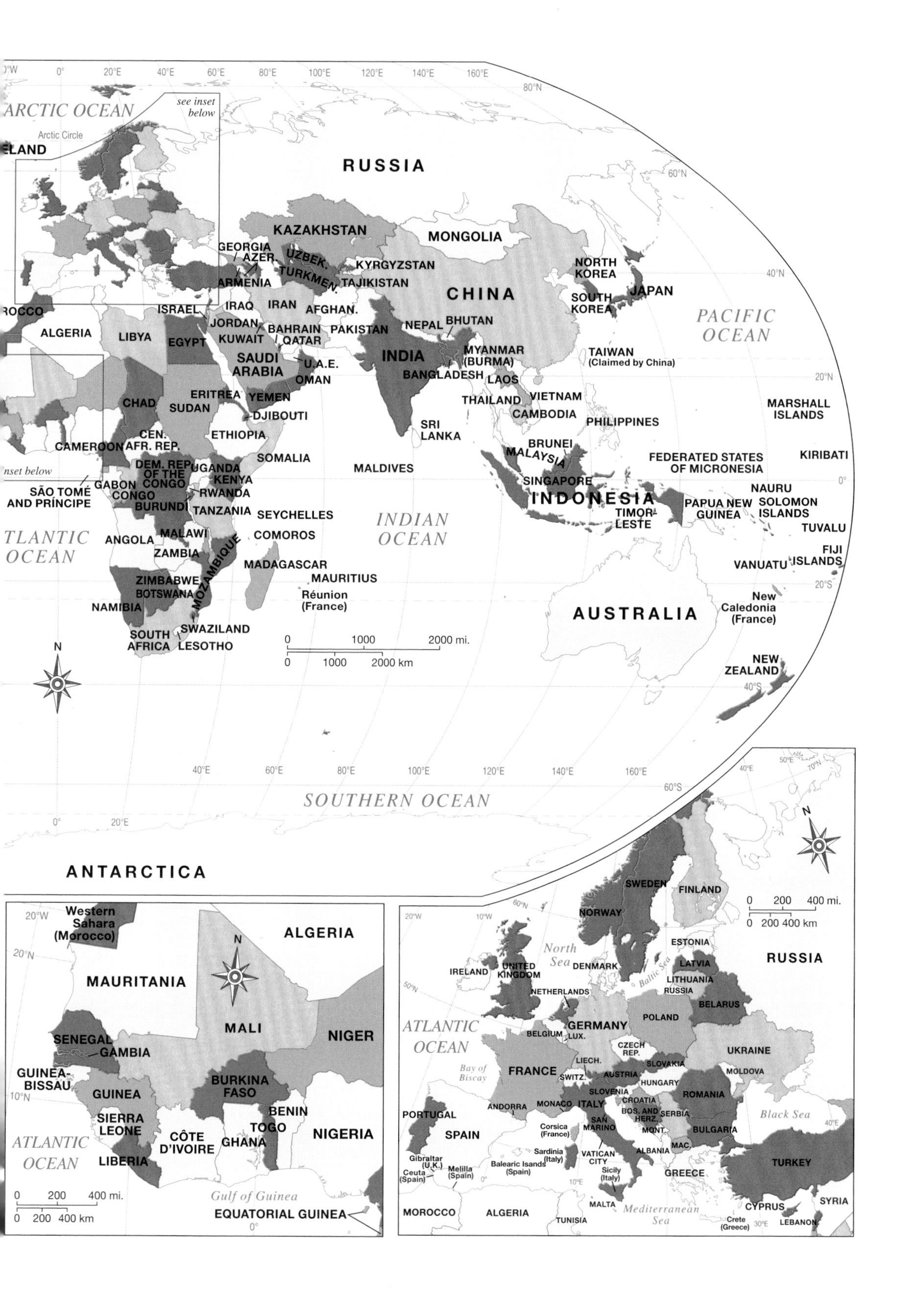

ARCTIC OCEAN
see inset below
RUSSIA
KAZAKHSTAN
MONGOLIA
GEORGIA
AZER.
ARMENIA
UZBEK.
TURKMEN.
KYRGYZSTAN
TAJIKISTAN
NORTH KOREA
SOUTH KOREA
JAPAN
CHINA
ISRAEL
IRAQ
IRAN
AFGHAN.
JORDAN
BAHRAIN
KUWAIT
QATAR
PAKISTAN
NEPAL
BHUTAN
ALGERIA
LIBYA
EGYPT
SAUDI ARABIA
U.A.E.
OMAN
INDIA
BANGLADESH
MYANMAR (BURMA)
LAOS
TAIWAN (Claimed by China)
PACIFIC OCEAN
CHAD
SUDAN
ERITREA
YEMEN
DJIBOUTI
THAILAND
VIETNAM
CAMBODIA
PHILIPPINES
MARSHALL ISLANDS
CEN. AFR. REP.
CAMEROON
ETHIOPIA
SOMALIA
SRI LANKA
BRUNEI
MALAYSIA
FEDERATED STATES OF MICRONESIA
KIRIBATI
DEM. REP. OF THE CONGO
UGANDA
KENYA
RWANDA
BURUNDI
GABON
CONGO
SÃO TOMÉ AND PRÍNCIPE
MALDIVES
SINGAPORE
INDONESIA
NAURU
PAPUA NEW GUINEA
SOLOMON ISLANDS
TIMOR-LESTE
TUVALU
TANZANIA
SEYCHELLES
COMOROS
INDIAN OCEAN
ATLANTIC OCEAN
ANGOLA
MALAWI
ZAMBIA
MOZAMBIQUE
MADAGASCAR
MAURITIUS
Réunion (France)
FIJI ISLANDS
VANUATU
ZIMBABWE
BOTSWANA
NAMIBIA
SOUTH AFRICA
SWAZILAND
LESOTHO
AUSTRALIA
New Caledonia (France)
NEW ZEALAND
0 1000 2000 mi.
0 1000 2000 km
SOUTHERN OCEAN
ANTARCTICA
Western Sahara (Morocco)
ALGERIA
MAURITANIA
MALI
NIGER
SENEGAL
GAMBIA
GUINEA-BISSAU
GUINEA
BURKINA FASO
BENIN
SIERRA LEONE
TOGO
CÔTE D'IVOIRE
GHANA
NIGERIA
LIBERIA
Gulf of Guinea
EQUATORIAL GUINEA
0 200 400 mi.
0 200 400 km
SWEDEN
FINLAND
NORWAY
ESTONIA
RUSSIA
North Sea
IRELAND
UNITED KINGDOM
DENMARK
Baltic Sea
LATVIA
LITHUANIA
RUSSIA
NETHERLANDS
BELARUS
POLAND
GERMANY
BELGIUM
LUX.
ATLANTIC OCEAN
CZECH REP.
UKRAINE
Bay of Biscay
FRANCE
LIECH.
SLOVAKIA
SWITZ.
AUSTRIA
MOLDOVA
HUNGARY
SLOVENIA
ROMANIA
CROATIA
ANDORRA
MONACO
ITALY
BOS. AND HERZ.
SERBIA
SAN MARINO
PORTUGAL
Corsica (France)
MONT.
BULGARIA
Black Sea
SPAIN
Sardinia (Italy)
VATICAN CITY
ALBANIA
MAC.
Gibraltar (U.K.)
Ceuta (Spain)
Melilla (Spain)
Balearic Isands (Spain)
Sicily (Italy)
GREECE
TURKEY
MOROCCO
ALGERIA
TUNISIA
MALTA
Mediterranean Sea
Crete (Greece)
CYPRUS
SYRIA
LEBANON
0 200 400 mi.
0 200 400 km

CHAPTER 1

Historical Background on the Arab-Israeli Six-Day War

VIEWPOINT 1

An Overview of the Arab-Israeli Six-Day War

Dictionary of the Israeli-Palestinian Conflict

The following viewpoint provides a summary of the Arab-Israeli Six-Day War. Fought from June 5th through June 10th 1967, the war resulted in a major victory for Israel over a coalition consisting of Egypt, Syria, Jordan, and Iraq, more than tripling Israel's size. It also confirmed Israel as a major regional military power and sent a message to neighboring Arab states that the nation would, at best, be extremely difficult to challenge on the battlefield in the future. Israel's occupation of territories that had previously been part of Arab states continues to be the key source of conflict in the Middle East. The related displacement of hundreds of thousands of Palestinian Arabs, which came along with those occupations, is another source of contention.

An Israeli army convoy moves through the Sinai Desert on June 8, 1967, as an open Israeli truck transports captured Egyptian soldiers to a prisoner of war camp. (© **Popperfoto/ Getty Images.**)

SOURCE. *Dictionary of the Israeli-Palestinian Conflict*. Belmont, CA: The Gale Group, 2005, pp. 33–35.

On 25 January 1967, the Israeli-Syrian mixed armistice commission convened, after an eight-year hiatus, and published a communiqué according to which the two parties had reached an agreement meant to prevent any hostile or aggressive action. On 7 April, in reprisal for Syrian artillery barrages on kibbutzim [communal farmers] in the north of Galilee, Israeli planes conducted a raid on the Golan, in the course of which six Syrian MiGs [fighter aircrafts] were downed. On 13 May, Soviet intelligence informed Cairo and Damascus that the Israelis were massing troops on the Syrian frontier. In the context of the Egyptian-Syrian defense pact, Egyptian president Gamal Abdel Nasser decided to mobilize his army. The following day, several Egyptian units left Cairo for the Sinai.

On 15 May, the anniversary date of the founding of Israel, the general staff of the Israel Defense Force (IDF) put on an impressive military parade. The day after, Syrian and Egyptian forces were put on high alert. On 19 May, at the request of the Egyptian government, the United Nations (UN) withdrew its troops, on duty since the end of the Suez-Sinai War of 1956, from Sinai and the Gaza Strip. On 20 May, Israel mobilized a part of its reserves. The next day, Egypt banned Israeli shipping in the Straits of Tiran, leading to a protest on the part of the United States, which declared the blockade of the Gulf of Aqaba illegal. With tension between Egypt and Israel at its apogee, on 25 May, Egyptian, Syrian, and Jordanian army divisions approached their respective frontiers with Israel. On 30 May, before the cameras of Egyptian television, King Hussein of Jordan signed a mutual defense pact with Egypt, according to which the Jordanian army would pass under Egyptian command in case of war. On 2 June, faced with Arab military preparations openly aimed at the Jewish state, Israeli prime minister Levi Eshkol ceded the portfolio of defense to Moshe Dayan. The next day, France and the United States decreed an embargo on arms shipments to the Middle East. On 4 June, Iraq joined the Syrian-Jordanian-Egyptian military alliance.

The Conflict Escalates

On the morning of 5 June 1967, Yitzhak Rabin, army chief-of-staff of the IDF, flanked by Generals Ezer Weizman and Haim Bar-Lev, unleashed a simultaneous attack against Egypt and Jordan. In a few hours, Israeli aircraft annihilated practically all of the Egyptian air force, surprised on the ground, and 416 Egyptian, Syrian, and Jordanian planes were destroyed. Sudan, Saudi Arabia, Algeria, and Yemen, in solidarity with the Arab countries, declared war on Israel. Egypt, Syria, Algeria, Yemen, Iraq, and Sudan broke off diplomatic relations with the United States, then with Great Britain. On 6 June, the U.S. ship *Liberty* was attacked by the Israelis, who claimed they had mistaken it for an Egyptian craft. Believing this to be Soviet aggression, U.S. president Lyndon Johnson ordered the U.S. fleet on high alert, while the U.S. Sixth Fleet approached the combat zone. On the same day, the UN Security Council unanimously passed a resolution demanding an immediate cease-fire. The next day, concluding its takeover of the West Bank, which had been under Jordanian control since 1948, Israeli troops, under the command of General Uzi Narkiss, penetrated into East Jerusalem. On the Egyptian front, Israeli troops were closing in on the Suez Canal. On 8 June, the UN Security Council unanimously adopted a resolution, again insisting on an immediate cease-fire. The Soviet Union and countries in its orbit, with the exception of Rumania, broke off diplomatic relations with Israel. Israel then attacked and captured the Golan region, and on 10 June, Syria

> The Israeli army had defeated the Egyptian, Jordanian, and Syrian armies in six days, Israel more than tripling its territorial area.

accepted a cease-fire. Movements of the U.S. Sixth Fleet, misinterpreted by the Soviet general staff, led to a state of high tension between Washington and Moscow, but this scare ended after only a few hours.

The Israeli army had defeated the Egyptian, Jordanian, and Syrian armies in six days, Israel more than tripling its territorial area by the occupation of the West Bank (which included East Jerusalem), a part of the Golan Heights, the Sinai Desert, and the Gaza Strip. Israeli military leaders judged now that they had acquired the strategic "depth" necessary to assure the security of Israel, while the ultra-orthodox movements perceived the victory of the IDF as the messianic expression of political Judaism. On 12 June, in the army's orders of the day, the chief-of-staff, Yitzhak Rabin, saluted the "unification and liberation of Jerusalem," and celebrated the victory of the "sons of light" over those who "wanted to cover the country with darkness." On 14 June, the UN Security Council adopted Resolution 237, recommending Israel respect international conventions concerning the treatment of prisoners of war and the protection of civilians in time of war. On 19 June, U.S. President Lyndon Johnson proposed a peace plan for the Middle East. Four days later, after his meeting with Johnson, Soviet prime minister Alexis Kosygin published a communiqué backing a peace plan in the Middle East, specifying that the "rapid withdrawal of Israeli troops is the key to the reestablishment of peace." On 27 June, the Israeli Knesset voted to annex the Arab part of Jerusalem. On 29 August, the leaders of Arab states, meeting in Khartoum, reaffirmed their will to continue the war against Israel with statements such as "no to peace, no to negotiations, no to recognition of Israel." The oil-producing states decided to aid Egypt financially. On 22 November, the UN Security Council unanimously adopted Resolution 242, requiring Israel to evacuate the occupied territories, in exchange for a cessation of the state of belligerence.

Photo on previous pages: The wreckage of an Egyptian Air Force jet is inspected by Israeli soldiers and observers following attacks by Israeli aircraft in June 1967. The Egyptian military suffered many losses during the six days of the war. (© **AP Images.**)

The Israeli Foreign Minister Justifies His Country's Attacks to the United Nations

Abba Eban

In the following viewpoint, Abba Eban speaks to the United Nations (UN) in hopes of explaining Israel's actions in launching the first attacks in the Six-Day War. Eban emphasizes the need for Israel to protect its rights as a sovereign nation, including the right to trade freely with other powers. He claims that Egypt impinged upon those rights by closing trade routes in the Straits of Tiran. Eban also reports some surprise that Israel's attempts to defend itself have not received more support from other nations or the UN. He hopes that Arab states will start to understand that Israel is now an established Middle Eastern power. Eban served as Israel's foreign minister as well as its ambassador to the United Nations in 1967.

SOURCE. Abba Eban, "Statement to the Security Council by Foreign Minister Eban," Israel Ministry of Foreign Affairs online, June 6, 1967. www.mfa.gov.il.

I thank you, Mr. President, for giving me this opportunity to address the Council. I have just come from Jerusalem to tell the [United Nations] Security Council that Israel, by its independent effort and sacrifice, has passed from serious danger to successful resistance.

Two days ago Israel's condition caused much concern across the humane and friendly world. Israel had reached a sombre hour. Let me try to evoke the point at which our fortunes stood.

The Threat to Israel

An army, greater than any force ever assembled in history in Sinai, had massed against Israel's southern frontier. Egypt had dismissed the United Nations forces which symbolized the international interest in the maintenance of peace in our region. [President of Egypt Gamal Abdal] Nasser had provocatively brought five infantry divisions and two armored divisions up to our very gates; 80,000 men and 900 tanks were poised to move.

A special striking force, comprising an armored division with at least 200 tanks, was concentrated against Eilat at the Negev's southern tip. Here was a clear design to cut the southern Negev off from the main body of our State. For Egypt had openly proclaimed that Eilat did not form part of Israel and had predicted that Israel itself would soon expire. The proclamation was empty; the prediction now lies in ruin. While the main brunt of the hostile threat was focused on the southern front, an alarming plan of encirclement was underway. With Egypt's initiative and guidance, Israel was already being strangled in its maritime approaches to the whole eastern half of the world. For sixteen years, Israel had been illicitly denied passage in the Suez Canal, despite the Security Council's decision of 1 September 1951 [Resolution 95 (1951)]. And now the creative enterprise of ten patient years which had opened an international route across the Strait of Tiran and the Gulf of Aqaba had been suddenly and arbitrarily choked. Israel was and is breathing only with a single lung.

Jordan had been intimidated, against its better interest, into joining a defense pact. It is not a defense pact at all: it is an aggressive pact, of which I saw the consequences with my own eyes yesterday in the shells falling upon institutions of health and culture in the City of Jerusalem. Every house and street in Jerusalem now came into the range of fire as a result of Jordan's adherence to this pact; so also did the crowded and pathetically narrow coastal strip in which so much of Israel's life and population is concentrated.

Attacks from Jordan

Iraqi troops reinforced Jordanian units in areas immediately facing vital and vulnerable Israel communication centers. Expeditionary forces from Algeria and Kuwait had reached Egyptian territory. Nearly all the Egyptian forces which had been attempting the conquest of the Yemen had been transferred to the coming assault upon Israel. Syrian units, including artillery, overlooked the Israel villages in the Jordan Valley. Terrorist troops came regularly into our territory to kill, plunder and set off explosions; the most recent occasion was five days ago.

In short, there was peril for Israel wherever it looked. . . . And Israel faced this danger alone.

In short, there was peril for Israel wherever it looked. Its manpower had been hastily mobilized. Its economy and commerce were bearing with feeble pulses. Its streets were dark and empty. There was an apocalyptic air of approaching peril. And Israel faced this danger alone.

We were buoyed up by an unforgettable surge of public sympathy across the world. The friendly Governments expressed the rather ominous hope that Israel

An Israeli officer patrols the streets of Jerusalem during the Six-Day War. The ancient holy city had strategic and symbolic significance for all sides involved in the conflict. (© **Stefan Tyszko/Getty Images.**)

would manage to live, but the dominant theme of our condition was danger and solitude.

Now there could be no doubt about what was intended for us. With my very ears I heard President Nasser's speech on 26 May. He said:

> We intend to open a general assault against Israel. This will be total war. Our basic aim will be to destroy Israel.

On 2 June, the Egyptian Commander in Sinai, General Mortagi, published his Order of the Day, calling on his troops to wage a war of destruction against Israel. Here, then, was a systematic, overt, proclaimed design at politicide, the murder of a State.

The policy, the arms, the men had all been brought together, and the State thus threatened with collective assault was itself the last sanctuary of a people which had seen six million of its sons exterminated by a more powerful dictator two decades before.

The question then widely asked in Israel and across the world was whether we had not already gone beyond the utmost point of danger. Was there any precedent in world history, for example, for a nation passively to suffer the blockade of its only southern port, involving nearly all its vital fuel, when such acts of war, legally and internationally, have always invited resistance? This was a most unusual patience. It existed because we had acceded to the suggestion of some of the maritime States that we give them scope to concert their efforts in order to find an international solution which would ensure the maintenance of free passage in the Gulf of Aqaba for ships of all nations and of all flags.

As we pursued this avenue of international solution, we wished the world to have no doubt about our readiness to exhaust every prospect, however fragile, of a diplomatic solution—and some of the prospects that were suggested were very fragile indeed.

Attacks from Egypt

But as time went on, there was no doubt that our margin of general security was becoming smaller and smaller. Thus, on the morning of 5 June, when Egyptian forces engaged us by air and land, bombarding the villages of Kissufim, Nahal-Oz and Ein Hashelosha, we knew that our limit of safety had been reached, and perhaps passed. In accordance with its inherent right of self-defense as formulated in Article 51 of the United Nations Charter, Israel responded defensively in full strength. Never in the history of nations has armed force been used in a more righteous or compelling cause.

Even when engaged with Egyptian forces, we still hoped to contain the conflict. Egypt was overtly bent on our destruction, but we still hoped that others would not join the aggression. Prime Minister Eshkol, who for weeks had carried the heavy burden of calculation and decision, published and conveyed a message to other neighboring States proclaiming:

> We shall not attack any country unless it opens war on us. Even now, when the mortars speak, we have not given up our quest for peace. We strive to repel all menace of terrorism and any danger of aggression to ensure our security and our legitimate rights.

In accordance with this same policy of attempting to contain the conflict, yesterday I invited General Bull, the [Norwegian] Chief of Staff of the Truce Supervision Organization, to inform the heads of the Jordanian State that Israel had no desire to expand the conflict beyond the unfortunate dimensions that it had already assumed and that if Israel were not attacked on the Jordan side, it would not attack and would act only in self-defence. It reached my ears that this message had been duly and faithfully conveyed and received. Nevertheless, Jordan decided to join the Egyptian posture against Israel and opened artillery attacks across the whole long frontier, including Jerusalem. Those attacks are still in progress.

Syrian Bombs Pose a Threat

To the appeal of Prime Minister Eshkol to avoid any further extension of the conflict, Syria answered at 12.25 yesterday morning by bombing Megiddo from the air and bombing Degania at 12.40 with artillery fire and kibbutz Ein Hammifrats and Kurdani with long-range guns. But Jordan embarked on a much more total assault by artillery and aircraft along the entire front, with special emphasis on Jerusalem, to whose dangerous and noble ordeal yesterday I come to bear personal witness.

There has been bombing of houses; there has been a hit on the great new National Museum of Art; there has been a hit on the University and on Shaare Zedek, the first hospital ever to have been established outside the ancient walls. Is this not an act of vandalism that deserves the condemnation of all mankind? And in the Knesset [legislature] building, whose construction had been movingly celebrated by the entire democratic world ten months ago, the Israel Cabinet and Parliament met under heavy gunfire, whose echoes mingled at the end of our meeting with Hatikvah, the anthem of hope.

Thus throughout the day and night of 5 June, the Jordan which we had expressly invited to abstain from needless slaughter became, to our surprise, and still remains, the most intense of all the belligerents; and death and injury, as so often in history, stalk Jerusalem's streets. . . .

We have lived through three dramatic weeks. Those weeks, I think, have brought into clear view the main elements of tension and also the chief promise of relaxed tension in the future. The first link in the chain was the series of sabotage acts emanating from Syria. In October of 1966, the Security Council was already seized of this problem, and a majority of its member States found it possible and necessary to draw attention to the Syrian Government's responsibility for altering that situation. Scarcely a day passed without a mine, a bomb, a hand-grenade or a mortar exploding on Israel's soil, sometimes with lethal or crippling effects, always with an unsettling psychological influence. In general, fourteen or fifteen such incidents would accumulate before a response was considered necessary, and this ceaseless accumulation of terrorist sabotage incidents in the name of what was called "popular war," together with responses which in the long run sometimes became inevitable, were for a long period the main focus of tension in the Middle East.

But then there came a graver source of tension in mid-May, when abnormal troop concentrations were observed in the Sinai Peninsula. For the ten years of relative stability beginning with March 1957 and ending with May 1967, the Sinai Desert had been free of Egyptian troops. In other words, a natural geographic barrier, a largely uninhabited space, separated the main forces of the two sides. It is true that in terms of sovereignty and law, any State has a right to put its armies in any part of its territory that it chooses. This, however, is not a legal question: it is a political and a security question.

> Massive armies in close proximity to each other, against a background of a doctrine of belligerency and accompanying threats . . . constitute an inflammatory situation.

Armies Face-to-Face

Experience in many parts of the world, not least in our own, demonstrates that massive armies in close proximity to each other, against a background of a doctrine of belligerency and accompanying threats by one army to annihilate the other, constitute an inflammatory situation.

We were puzzled in Israel by the relative lack of preoccupation on the part of friendly Governments and international agencies with this intense concentration which found its reflection in precautionary concentrations on our side. My Government proposed, I think at least two weeks ago, the concept of a parallel and reciprocal reduction of forces on both sides of the frontier. We elicited no response, and certainly no action.

To these grave sources of tension—the sabotage and terrorist movement, emanating mostly from Syria, and the heavy troop concentrations accompanied by dire, apocalyptic threats in Sinai—there was added in the third week of May the most electric shock of all, namely the closure of the international waterway consisting of the Strait of Tiran and the Gulf of Aqaba. It is not difficult, I think, to understand why this incident had a more drastic impact than any other. In 1957 the maritime nations, within the framework of the United Nations General Assembly, correctly enunciated the doctrine of free and innocent passage through the Strait.

Now, when that doctrine was proclaimed—and incidentally, not challenged by the Egyptian representative at that time—it was little more than an abstract principle for the maritime world. For Israel it was a great but still unfulfilled prospect; it was not yet a reality. But during the ten years in which we and the other States of the maritime community have relied upon that doctrine and upon established usage, the principle has become a reality consecrated by hundreds of sailings under dozens of flags and the establishment of a whole complex of commerce and industry and communication. A new dimension has been added to the map of the world's communications, and on that dimension we have constructed Israel's bridge towards the friendly States of Asia and Africa, a network of relationships which is the chief pride of Israel in the second decade of its independence.

Blocking Israel's Ports to the East

All this, then, had grown up as an effective usage under the United Nations flag. Does Mr. Nasser really think that he can come upon the scene in ten minutes and cancel the established legal usage and interests of ten years?

There was in this wanton act a quality of malice. For surely the closing of the Strait of Tiran gave no benefit whatever to Egypt except the perverse joy of inflicting injury on others. It was an anarchic act, because it showed a total disregard for the law of nations, the application of which in this specific case had not been challenged for ten years. And it was, in the literal sense, an act of arrogance, because there are other nations in Asia and East Africa that trade with the Port of Eilat, as they have every right to do, through the Strait of Tiran and across the Gulf of Aqaba. Other sovereign States from Japan to Ethiopia, from Thailand to Uganda, from Cambodia to Madagascar, have a sovereign right to decide for themselves whether they wish or do not wish to trade with Israel. These countries are not colonies of Cairo. They can trade with Israel or not trade with Israel as they wish, and President Nasser is not the policeman of other African and Asian States.

Here then was a wanton intervention in the sovereign rights of other States in the eastern half of the world to decide for themselves whether or not they wish to establish trade relations with either or both of the two ports at the head of the Gulf of Aqaba.

When we examine, then, the implications of this act, we have no cause to wonder that the international shock was great. There was another reason too for that shock. Blockades have traditionally been regarded, in the pre-Charter parlance, as acts of war. To blockade, after all, is to attempt strangulation; and sovereign States are entitled not to have their trade strangled. To understand how the State of Israel felt, one has merely to look around this table and imagine, for example, a foreign Power forcibly closing New York or Montreal, Boston or Marseille, Toulon or Copenhagen, Rio or Tokyo or Bombay harbor. How would your Governments react? What would you do? How long would you wait?

But Israel waited because of its confidence that the other maritime Powers and countries interested in this new trading pattern would concert their influence in order to re-establish a legal situation and to liquidate this blockade. We concerted action with them not because Israel's national interest was here abdicated. There will not be, there cannot be, an Israel without Eilat. We cannot be expected to return to a dwarfed stature, with our face to the Mediterranean alone. In law and in history, peace and blockades have never co-existed. How could it be expected that the blockade of Eilat and a relaxation of tension in the Middle East could ever be brought into harmony?

These then were the three main elements in the tension: the sabotage movement; the blockade of the port; and, perhaps more imminent than anything else, this

The Founding of Israel

The modern nation of Israel first appeared in 1948. It was carved out of territory on the eastern edge of the Mediterranean Sea known for centuries under the generic name of Palestine. Jews recognized the area as their traditional homeland, and it was the site of the biblical Kingdom of Israel.

Activist European Jews, members of the modern Zionist movement, began establishing Jewish settlements in Palestine around the beginning of the twentieth century. After World War I (1914–1918), Palestine passed from Turkish to British control, with the area now known as the Palestinian Mandate. The British had already made clear their support for a Jewish state in the Balfour Declaration of 1917, which also urged that the rights of non-Jews in the region be respected. As more Jews moved to the Mandate in the 1930s, some to escape persecution in Nazi Germany, the Peel Commission of 1937 proposed the creation of both a Jewish and a Palestinian Arab state. The proposal was ultimately rejected, and unhappy Arabs began to engage in violence against what many Arabs saw as overly assertive Jewish settlers.

After World War II (1939–1945), and in the face of more Jewish immigration and localized violence, the British made plans to leave Palestine and turned its future over to the United Nations (UN). In late 1947, the UN voted to approve a new proposal for two states, and in 1948 Jewish leaders took advantage of the opportunity to declare national independence in a ceremony held on May 14th. Arab leaders, unhappy with the UN vote and with partition plans, started the First Arab-Israeli War soon after. The coalition of Egypt, Jordan, Syria, Lebanon, Iraq, Libya, and Sudan was quickly defeated by Israel, which refers to the conflict as its war for independence. Meanwhile, many of the world's nations had already granted the new state of Israel official diplomatic recognition.

Israel's first borders were established in 1949 in various agreements with Arab powers that insisted the specifics be open to future negotiations. While Israel ended up being bigger than the 1947 UN proposal suggested, the Sinai Peninsula and Gaza Strip remained under Egyptian control, the Golan Heights belonged to Syria, and the West Bank was governed by the Kingdom of Jordan. Jordan also controlled East Jerusalem, a city now split. Meanwhile, some 750,000 Palestinian Arabs were displaced, both voluntarily and involuntarily.

vast and purposeful encirclement movement, against the background of an authorized presidential statement announcing that the objective of the encirclement was to bring about the destruction and the annihilation of a sovereign State.

These acts taken together—the blockade, the dismissal of the United Nations Emergency Force, and the heavy concentration in Sinai—effectively disrupted the status quo which had ensured a relative stability on the Egyptian-Israel frontier for ten years. . . .

> There will never be a Middle East without an independent and sovereign State of Israel in its midst.

The central point remains the need to secure an authentic intellectual recognition by our neighbors of Israel's deep roots in the Middle Eastern reality. There is an intellectual tragedy in the failure of Arab leaders to come to grips, however reluctantly, with the depth and authenticity of Israel's roots in the life, the history, the spiritual experience and the culture of the Middle East.

Proposals for a Peaceful Future

This, then, is the first axiom. A much more conscious and uninhibited acceptance of Israel's statehood is an axiom requiring no demonstration, for there will never be a Middle East without an independent and sovereign State of Israel in its midst.

The second principle must be that of the peaceful settlement of disputes. The Resolution thus adopted falls within the concept of the peaceful settlement of disputes. I have already said that much could be done if the Governments of the area would embark much more on direct contacts. They must find their way to each other. After all, when there is conflict between them they come together face to face. Why should they not come together face to face to solve the conflict? And perhaps on some occasions it would not be a bad idea to have the solution before, and therefore instead of, the conflict.

When the Council discusses what is to happen after the cease-fire, we hear many formulas: back to 1956, back to 1948—I understand our neighbors would wish to turn the clock back to 1947. The fact is, however, that most clocks move forward and not backward, and this, I think, should be the case with the clock of Middle Eastern peace—not backward to belligerency, but forward to peace.

The point was well made this evening by the representative of Argentina, who said: the cease-fire should be followed immediately by the most intensive efforts to bring about a just and lasting peace in the Middle East. In a similar sense, the representative of Canada warned us against merely reproducing the old positions of conflict, without attempting to settle the underlying issues of Arab-Israel co-existence. After all, many things in recent days have been mixed up with each other. Few things are what they were. And in order to create harmonious combinations of relationships, it is inevitable that the States should come together in negotiation.

Another factor in the harmony that we would like to see in the Middle East relates to external Powers. From these, and especially from the greatest amongst them, the small States of the Middle East—and most of them are small—ask for a rigorous support, not for individual States, but for specific principles; not to be for one State against other States, but to be for peace against war, for free commerce against belligerency, for the pacific settlement of disputes against violent irredentist threats; in other words, to exercise an even-handed support for the integrity and independence of States and for the rights of States under the Charter of the United Nations and other sources of international law.

There are not two categories of States. The United Arab Republic, Iraq, Syria, Jordan, Lebanon—not one of these has a single ounce or milligram of statehood which does not adhere in equal measures to Israel itself. . . .

I would say in conclusion that these are, of course, still grave times. And yet they may perhaps have a fortunate issue. This could be the case if those who for some reason decided so violently, three weeks ago, to disrupt the status quo would ask themselves what the results and benefits have been. As he looks around him at the arena of battle, at the wreckage of planes and tanks, at the collapse of intoxicated hopes, might not an Egyptian ruler ponder whether anything was achieved by that disruption? What has it brought but strife, conflict with other powerful interests, and the stem criticism of progressive men throughout the world?

I think that Israel has in recent days proved its steadfastness and vigor. It is now willing to demonstrate its instinct for peace. Let us build a new system of relationships from the wreckage of the old. Let us discern across the darkness the vision of a better and a brighter dawn.

VIEWPOINT 3

United Nations Security Council Resolution 242

United Nations Security Council

The following viewpoint is the text from the United Nations' Security Council Resolution 242. Agreed upon unanimously by the Security Council in November 1967, it calls for a peaceful end to Middle East conflicts and for nations to respect one another's borders. It also calls for Israel to remove its armed forces from territories occupied during the Six-Day War. Israel, Arab states, and Palestinian groups have mostly used the resolution as the basis for new negotiations, and they have adopted their own interpretations. Israel, for example, believes the nation was not asked to withdraw from all the territories occupied in the Six-Day War, only some of them, while the Palestine Liberation Organization rejected the resolution entirely until 1993, when it officially recognized Israel's right to exist.

SOURCE. "United Nations Security Council Resolution 242," United Nations Security Council online, November 22, 1967. http://daccess-dds-ny.un.org.

Resolution 242 (1967)
of 22 November 1967

The Security Council,

Expressing its continuing concern with the grave situation in the Middle East,

Emphasizing the inadmissibility of the acquisition of territory by war and the need to work for a just and lasting peace in which every State in the area can live in security,

> The fulfilment of Charter principles requires the establishment of a just and lasting peace in the Middle East.

Emphasizing further that all Member States in their acceptance of the Charter of the United Nations have undertaken a commitment to act in accordance with Article 2 of the Charter,

1. *Affirms* that the fulfilment of Charter principles requires the establishment of a just and lasting peace in the Middle East which should include the application of both the following principles:

    (i) Withdrawal of Israel armed forces from territories occupied in the recent conflict;

    (ii) Termination of all claims or states of belligerency and respect for and acknowledgement of the sovereignty, territorial integrity and political independence of every State in the area and their right to live in peace within secure and recognized boundaries free from threats or acts of force;

2. *Affirms further* the necessity

    (*a*) For guaranteeing freedom of navigation through international waterways in the area;

    (*b*) For achieving a just settlement of the refugee problem;

CHANGING TERRITORY BEFORE AND AFTER THE SIX-DAY WAR

1967

- Israel before the Six-Day War
- Under Israeli control after the Six-Day War

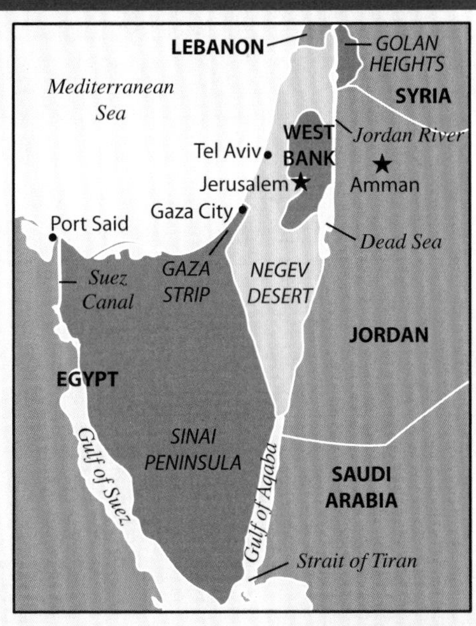

Today

- Israel
- Full or partial Palestinian control
- Occupied by Israel

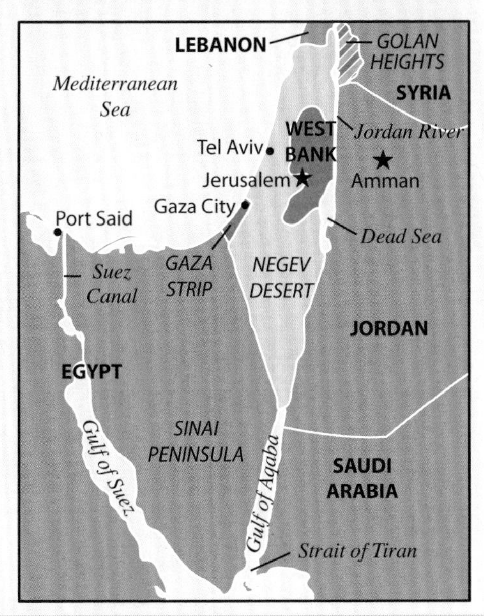

0 100 mi
0 100 km

Taken from: Sam Roberts, "1967: The Six-Day War," *New York Times Upfront*, April 16, 2007. teacher.scholastic.com

Palestinian families move out of the Jewish Quarter in Jerusalem in June 1967. The Palestinian leadership rejected UN Security Council Resolution 242. (© **Rolls Press/ Popperfoto/Getty Images.**)

(*c*) For guaranteeing the territorial inviolability and political independence of every State in the area, through measures including the establishment of demilitarized zones;

3. *Requests* the Secretary-General to designate a Special Representative to proceed to the Middle East to establish and maintain contacts with the States concerned in order to promote agreement and assist efforts to

achieve a peaceful and accepted settlement in accordance with the provisions and principles in this resolution;

4. *Requests* the Secretary-General to report to the Security Council on the progress of the efforts of the Special Representative as soon as possible.

Adopted unanimously at the 1382nd meeting.

Israel Became a Major Regional Power Due to the 1967 War

Abraham Rabinovich

In the following viewpoint, Abraham Rabinovich examines how Israel's victory in the Six-Day War changed the nation and its status in the world. The victory made the nation more attractive for both immigration and outside investment and support. Meanwhile, Rabinovich argues, the war convinced Arab nations that Israel could not be defeated militarily, and he examines how in the years since 1967, Arab nations have successively made their peace with the Israeli state. Rabinovich is a journalist and author of *The Yom Kippur War* and *The Battle for Jerusalem*.

Forty years after [2007] the Six Day War, the consequences of Israel's extraordinary victory, for good and ill, have still not sorted themselves out.

SOURCE. Abraham Rabinovich, "Six Day War Established Israel's Place in Middle East," *Hartford Courant* online, June 3, 2007. http://articles.courant.com.

Israel was a tiny (8,000-square-mile) Middle East backwater in 1967 with a population of 2.6 million surrounded by a hostile Arab world of some 80 million. This disparity seemed to defy the natural order of things and it was a virtual Arab consensus that the Jewish state would fall, sooner rather than later. In Israel itself, the enthusiasm and energy that marked the founding of the state 19 years before out of the ashes of the Holocaust had been dimmed by the petty problems of a country with a massive defense burden and a lame economy. A standing joke was "would the last person leaving Lod (International) Airport please turn off the lights."

It was the Soviet Union, for reasons never adequately clarified, that lit the fuse that would transform the region. In mid-May 1967, it warned that Israel was massing troops in the north in preparation for an attack on Syria. Israeli Prime Minister Levi Eshkol offered to personally tour the north with the Soviet ambassador to show it wasn't true. The ambassador declined.

There had been small-scale skirmishing between Israel and Syria over the headwaters of the Jordan and Israeli leaders had issued warnings, but there was no massing of troops. Egyptian President Gamal Abdel Nasser, the leading figure in the Arab world, felt impelled to come to Syria's aid after the Soviet warning by moving his armored divisions through the Sinai desert toward Israel. With a hostile army deploying on its border, Israel mobilized its reserves.

Nothing happened for more than two weeks. But mobilization of much of its manpower had paralyzed the Israeli economy and Jerusalem had to either stand down or strike. On the morning of June 5, Israeli planes, flying low to avoid radar, suddenly rose into the Egyptian skies. Within three hours, the Egyptian air force was destroyed. Shortly thereafter, the Jordanian, Syrian and part of the Iraqi air forces were gone too.

Israeli armor broke through Egyptian defenses in Sinai and reached the Sinai Canal. On the third day of the war, the West Bank and Jordanian Jerusalem fell to Israel. Syria's Golan Heights followed. The Arab world was stunned, Israel euphoric.

Photo on previous page: Israeli soldiers guard a group of Egyptians in Gaza Strip during the Six-Day War. The successful show of force changed neighboring countries' opinions of Israel. (© **David Rubinger/Time & Life Pictures/Getty Images.**)

Israel's New Status

The war catapulted Israel into a vibrant new era. Abrim with self-confidence and renewed energy, it attracted immigration from the West and more than a million immigrants from the Soviet Union. It attracted investments as well which funded a proliferation of hi-tech start-ups, surpassed in number only by the United States. Since 1967, Israel's population has tripled to 7.1 million (of whom 1.4 million are Israeli Arabs), its gross national product has grown by 630 percent and per capita income has almost tripled to $21,000.

A major result of the Six Day War was to persuade the Arab world that Israel was too strong to be defeated. Internalizing that view, Nasser's successor, Anwar Sadat, became in 1970 the first Arab leader to declare readiness to make peace with Israel if it withdrew from all territory it had captured in the Six Day War.

Israel insisted, however, on territorial changes. It took the 1973 Yom Kippur War to induce Israel to withdraw from all Egyptian territory and for Egypt to agree to peace without insisting on Israel's withdrawal on other fronts as well.

The Oslo Accords in 1993, marking the beginning of a political dialogue between Israel and the Palestinians, enabled Jordan to also make peace with Israel, without being accused of betraying the Palestinian cause. Other Arab countries, from Morocco to the Persian Gulf, opened a dialogue with Israel and some even established legations in Tel Aviv. In 2000, Syria announced its readiness for peace.

Although negotiations with Damascus broke down, virtually the entire Arab world now accepted the legitimacy, or at least the existence, of the Jewish state in its midst, something that would have been regarded as fantasy before the Six Day War.

Virtually the entire Arab world now accepted the legitimacy, or at least the existence, of the Jewish state in its midst.

However, inability to resolve the Palestinian problem, for which blame can be shared by Israel and the Palestinians themselves, threatens to unravel the grand hopes for a New Middle East that the war had set in motion. Increasing radicalization has brought to the Palestinian leadership a movement dedicated to Israel's destruction and Israel is at a loss at how to dismount safely from the Palestinian tiger it has been riding.

If there is an answer, it lies—as in 1967—in bold and imaginative leadership, but this time on the political playing field and not just in the Israeli camp.

VIEWPOINT 5

Palestinian Refugees

Anti-Defamation League

The problem of Palestinian refugees first appeared in the aftermath of the establishment of the state of Israel and the first Arab-Israeli War in 1948. It was compounded by the 1967 Six-Day War, which not only created more refugees, but also displaced once again some of those who were uprooted nearly twenty years earlier. The following selection is a report from the Anti-Defamation League, an American organization that combats anti-Semitism in particular and bigotry in general. It notes that the status of Palestinian refugees is complicated by the fact that neighboring Arab nations, except for Jordan, refused to integrate them into their own populations before 1967 and by the argument that many of them continue to insist they have a "right of return" to homes lost in 1948 or 1967. It also notes that many Jewish refugees were created by the hostility of Arab states toward the rise of Israel. Meanwhile, Israel rejects the right of return for Palestinians as well as complete responsibility for their welfare, favoring an international solution.

SOURCE. "Fortieth Anniversary of the Six Day War: Refugees," Anti-Defamation League online. http://adl.org.

The Palestinian refugee problem originated as a result of the 1948 Arab-Israeli war, when five Arab armies invaded the State of Israel just hours after it was established. During the ensuing war as many as 700,000 Palestinians fled their homes in the newly created state. Many of the Palestinians who fled did so voluntarily to avoid the ongoing war or at the urging of Arab leaders who promised that all who left would return after a quick Arab victory over the new Jewish state. Other Palestinians were forced to flee by individuals or groups fighting for Israel.

Of the Palestinians who left, one-third went to the West Bank, one-third to the Gaza Strip, and the remainder to Jordan, Lebanon and Syria. The Arab nations refused to absorb these Palestinians into their population and they were instead settled into refugee camps. Only Jordan's King Abdullah agreed to confer citizen-ship on the 200,000 Palestinian living in Jordan and the Jordan-controlled West Bank and East Jerusalem. In 1949, the United Nations Relief and Works Agency for Palestinian Refugees in the Near East (UNRWA) was created to oversee the economic integration of the refugees into these Arab countries. The Arab governments refused to consider integration, insisting that it would undermine the refugees' "right" to return to their homes in Palestine. UNRWA continues to operate, providing relief, health care, education and vocational training to the refugee populations in Jordan, Syria, Lebanon, the West Bank and Gaza Strip.

During the 1967 Six Day War, another estimated 250,000 Palestinians fled the West Bank and Gaza Strip with the arrival of Israeli forces. Some of these were people who had left their homes in Israel in 1948. These individuals are considered by the international community to be displaced persons, not refugees.

A Jewish refugee problem was also created with the establishment of the State of Israel. From 1948–1951

PALESTINIAN REFUGEES AS OF JANUARY 1, 2011

Nation or Region	Official Refugee Camps	Refugees in Camps	Total Refugees
Jordan	10	350,899	1,999,466
Gaza Strip	8	518,147	1,167,361
West Bank (Israel)	19	206,123	848,494
Syria	9	149,822	495,970
Lebanon	12	227,718	455,373
Totals	**58**	**1,452,709**	**4,966,664**

Taken from: United Nations Relief and Works Agency, "UNRWA In Figures: As of 1 January 2011," July 2011. www.unrwa.org.

as many as 800,000 Jews were expelled from their native Arab nations or forced to flee as a result of state-sponsored anti-Zionist violence. They left behind their property and the lives they had built in these lands over hundreds of years. As many as 500,000 of these refugees fled from Iraq, Tunisia, Syria, Egypt, Yemen, Algeria, Libya and Morocco and were absorbed into the new State of Israel. Others fled to Europe and North and South America where they were forced to rebuild their lives.

Tallying the number of individuals considered Palestinian refugees today is a matter of debate. UNRWA, which registers Palestinian refugees, claims that refugees and their descendants number five million, including: those who left Israel in 1948; those who left the West Bank and Gaza Strip in 1967; those who were abroad but were subsequently not allowed to return to Israel; and all of their descendants. UNRWA's statistics include those residing in Jordan, Lebanon, Syria, the West Bank and

Gaza Strip. (UNRWA's policy of including the children, grandchildren and great-grandchildren of those who left in 1948 and 1967 into the refugee population for demographic and aid purposes is not done for any other refugee group.) Israel believes the UNRWA statistics are exaggerated. Israel also strictly distinguishes "refugees" from "displaced persons" and from "expired permit Palestinians" who were abroad at the time the conflicts ensued and were not allowed to return.

Palestinian insistence that refugees must have a "right of return" to their former homes inside Israel, and that this "right" is founded in international law, is rejected by Israel. Israel denies that there is any foundation in international law for a Palestinian "right of return," and that the non-binding international resolutions on the issue call not for a "return" to Israel, but for a just resolution of the refugee problem. Israel also argues that a "return" is not viable for such a small state, given that the influx of millions of Palestinians into Israel would pose a threat to its national security and upset the country's demographic makeup. In the decades that the Palestine Liberation Organization (PLO) did not recognize Israel's right to exist and actively sought to bring about Israel's downfall and replace it with a Palestinian state, the "right of return" of Palestinian refugees was a rallying cry. In 1993, the PLO recognized Israel's right to exist and committed to a negotiating process to establish an independent Palestinian state alongside the State of Israel. Given this situation, world leaders, including President Bill Clinton and President George W. Bush, publicly stated that Palestinian refugees should rightly be resettled in a future Palestinian state.

> Israel maintains that it is not responsible for the Palestinian refugee problem [but] that on humanitarian grounds it would participate in an international effort to resolve the situation.

Many Palestinians were left without homes as a result of the war in 1967. Refugees continue to insist they have a "right of return" to their old homes. (© **AP Images.**)

Israel maintains that it is not responsible for the Palestinian refugee problem since it is the result of a war forced on Israel by invading Arab armies. However, Israel has stated that on humanitarian grounds it would participate in an international effort to resolve the situation. Such an effort would likely involve Palestinian refugees settling in a newly established state of Palestine, an international compensation fund, and individual cases of family reunification. Any international effort would also need to consider the situation of the 800,000 Jews who were expelled from their native Arab nations or forced to flee as a result of state-sponsored anti-Jewish violence following the founding of the State of Israel.

VIEWPOINT 6

The 1967 Arab-Israeli War Had Far-Reaching Implications

Ned Temko

In the following viewpoint, Ned Temko examines the 1967 war and its long-term legacies. Temko notes how the borders that were redrawn after the war as well as the status of Palestinian refugees continue to be major sources of conflict. While some of the territorial issues, such as the status of the Sinai Peninsula, were eventually resolved, Temko writes how control of Jerusalem and the West Bank of the Jordan River remain non-negotiable for Israelis. Meanwhile, the Palestinians and nations in the Arab world continue to call for their version of justice. Temko lives in the United Kingdom, where his articles frequently appear in newspapers such as *The Observer* and *The Guardian*. He is also a television commentator.

SOURCE. Ned Temko, "War Without End," *Observer*, May 5, 2007. http://guardian.co.uk.

The sirens sounded, gasped into silence as if some giant animal were catching its breath, then sounded again. It was a familiar dirge amid the weathered blocks of flats on the Mediterranean seafront of Tel Aviv [Israel] in the early months of 1967. Air-raid drills were just one sign of escalating tension between the precarious, teenage state of Israel and a coalition of surrounding Arab neighbours led by President Gamal Abdel-Nasser's Egypt.

Few Israelis doubted the wails of warning meant war. Few were confident it would end in victory.

But this time—on the morning of 5 June 1967—few Israelis doubted the wails of warning meant war. Few were confident it would end in victory. Fewer still felt that if victory did come, it would come easily, or soon. On the last score, they would be proven utterly and spectacularly wrong.

Within hours, Israeli jets would destroy virtually all Egypt's 450 combat aircraft on the ground. By the day's end, the Syrian air force would be similarly crippled.

A day later, Israeli troops were fighting their way across the concrete and barbed wire that divided the disputed holy city of Jerusalem into its Israeli-held west and its Jordanian-ruled east—and capturing Judaism's holiest site, the Western Wall, sole surviving remnant of the ancient Jewish temple. Ground fighting, often fierce, rumbled on for four more days, with Israel ultimately going on to capture the entire West Bank from Jordan on its eastern flank; Gaza and the Sinai desert from Egypt in the south; and the towering Golan Heights from Syria in the north.

The Human Cost

In barely 130 hours, the fighting was all over. Yet however quick, the war had not been bloodless. Israel lost about 1,100 dead, the Egyptians more than 10,000, the Syrians

2,500 and Jordan about 700. And some 300,000 Palestinians from the West Bank fled the fighting eastward into Jordan—in some cases 'double refugees', because they had also lost their homes in the fighting surrounding the establishment of Israel 20 years earlier.

It is now four decades since the Six-Day War, but its effects reverberate still—in Israel, the occupied Palestinian territories, the Middle East and the wider world. When [former British prime minister and Middle East peace diplomat] Tony Blair shuttles to Jerusalem and Ramallah and Cairo speaking of the urgency of getting Israeli-Palestinian peace talks back on track; when [US president] George Bush and [US secretary of state] Condoleezza Rice proclaim a commitment to the 'diplomatic road map'; when a Saudi-led Arab summit urges a 'land-for-peace' deal; or when [extremist Islamist organization] al-Qaeda propagandists cite 'Palestine' among the litany of grievances to recruit suicide bombers to pilot passenger planes into New York skyscrapers or blow up tube trains in London; all, in their own ways, are negotiating the unfinished business of six days of war in June 1967.

A New Nation

When the war broke out, Israel was barely 19 years old, and barely 10 miles wide at its narrowest point. There were none of the luxury hotels, pricey restaurants or all-night bars and clubs that today dot Tel Aviv's seafront; none of the hi-tech businesses that lie northwards up the coast. Israel's equivalent of the BBC [British Broadcasting Company] would not introduce television broadcasts until the following year.

The state had been established in 1948 on the back of a UN resolution partitioning British Mandate Palestine into two states: one a national home for the Jews, six million of whom had been murdered in [German dictator Adolf] Hitler's Holocaust, the other for Palestinian Arabs. The Arab states rejected the plan, and their armies invaded when Israel declared statehood. Israel survived, winning a protracted battle it called the War of Independence. In Arabic it is known, to this day, simply as *al naqba*—the catastrophe.

The Arab world—politically at least—was also unrecognisably different in the early days of June 1967. The Palestinian issue was, then as now, a central rallying cry. Hundreds of thousands of Palestinians, after all, had fled or been forced out of what became Israel in the 1948 war. But as an independent political voice, they were so feeble as to be barely audible, dismissed not only by Israel but by Arab kings and presidents whose own national interests, or pretensions to claim leadership of a wider nationalist cause, took precedence. The Palestine Liberation Organisation [PLO] existed. Yet it was a creature of Nasser and run by an acolyte named Ahmad Shukeiri.

Arab Political Intrigues

By the spring of 1967, Nasser—with his charismatic podium presence and Soviet-supplied military—was determined to fashion a powerful alliance of Israel's Arab neighbours to reverse once and for all the humiliation of 1948. He found an avid partner in another Kremlin ally, Syria's [leader] Hafez al-Assad, and a willing, if less eager, one in the pro-western King Hussein of Jordan. For months, tension had been mounting, with strikes and counter-strikes on Israel's borders. Whether either side truly wanted, or expected, full-scale war remains uncertain four decades later. What is clear is that each side, increasingly, became convinced the other was bent on confrontation.

In Israel, Prime Minister Levi Eshkol—a competent but colourless Labour successor to the country's founding leader, David Ben-Gurion—was so halting in his response to the rising tension that he was sowing

Photo on opposite page: On June 7, 1967, a group of Israeli paratroopers stands in front of the Wailing Wall in Jerusalem. Prior to the war, Israelis had not been able to enter this holy Jewish site. (© David Rubinger/Time & Life Pictures/Getty Images.)

something very near to panic among his generals. Addressing the nation on the radio in May, he fumbled at his notes, stumbled in his delivery and within days was forced to bring the eyepatched war veteran Moshe Dayan into his cabinet as defence minister in an emergency 'unity' government to steady the country's nerves.

In Egypt, Nasser was sabre-rattling, but had yet clearly to demonstrate that he was poised to move from rhetoric to battle. But in the final weeks of May he took a series of steps that were to make war inevitable. On the 16th, he demanded the removal of a UN buffer force deployed in the Sinai since the disastrous British-French-Israeli seizure of the Suez Canal in 1956. On 22 May, Nasser announced what amounted to a blockade of Israel, closing the Strait of Tiran and the top of the Red Sea to Israeli shipping. And he then ordered some 100,000 troops, with almost 1,000 tanks and 1,000 other armoured vehicles—well over half of his armed forces—into the Sinai, near Israel's southern border. At the month's end, he declared: 'The Arabs are arranged for battle. The critical hour has arrived.'

It was Israel, shortly after 7am on 5 June, that struck first, attacking and destroying Egypt's air force. When Jordanian troops and artillery joined the war from the east, and the Syrians from the Golan, Israel struck on both those fronts. And by 10 June, the fighting was over.

The next morning, Levi Eshkol's top aides were gathered in his office in a mood of relief, astonishment and celebration, when the Prime Minister walked in and—one of them later recalled—said: 'What are you so happy about?' In military terms, the victory had been extraordinary. Within the space of a week, a narrow, seaside Israel had tripled in size. Militarily and strategically, it had been transformed from precarious prey to regional superpower. 'Eshkol's mood was surprisingly sober,' the aide recounted. 'He saw that our political problems were only just beginning.'

New Territories

And they were. The initial hope among Israel's political leaders was that at least the bulk of land they had captured could be traded for treaties of peace with Egypt, Syria and Jordan. Yet there were early signs that they saw the prospect of a deal with Jordan—involving, as it did, the future of the West Bank and of Jerusalem—as by far the most complicated. Egypt's Sinai and the Syrian Golan were fairly sparsely populated. The only reason to hold on to them would be as a strategic buffer, a function the Israelis figured could be retained in a future land-for-peace deal by ensuring they were 'demilitarised'.

Jerusalem was different: it was Judaism's holiest site and ancient capital, for 19 years divided, now wholly under Israeli rule. The West Bank, too, had powerful historical resonance for Israelis. For the assertively Orthodox, a minority in Israel whose huge effect on settlement policy began in the months after the 1967 war, the attraction was particularly powerful: the place names of its towns and villages were part of the biblical narrative they read aloud each week in synagogue.

A year after the war, the first of the Jewish settlements on the West Bank had been approved.

But in the weeks after the war other secular Israelis also voted with their picnic baskets. They eagerly visited the undivided Jerusalem—with the area around the Western Wall and the ancient Jewish Quarter of the walled Old City soon cleared by Israeli bulldozers. They also visited not only West Bank cities with biblical echoes such as Hebron, but sites such as Gush Etzion, where Jewish residents were twice violently forced out, first in 1929 and then a week before the establishment of Israel in 1948.

The First of Many Jewish Settlements

A year after the war, the first of the Jewish settlements on the West Bank had been approved: at Gush Etzion and near Hebron. The decision came under a broadly secular Labour government, though amid pressure stoked by a burgeoning movement of Orthodox nationalist settlers known as Gush Emunim, the Bloc of the Faithful. Other settlements followed, particularly under Menachem Begin's right-wing Israeli government in the late Seventies and early Eighties. By then, the aim of the settlements was clear and openly stated: to underline Begin's determination to hold on to overall control of the West Bank under any future peace deal, and to rule out ever agreeing to a Palestinian state there.

In truth, though, whatever early hopes Israeli harboured for peace deals after the 1967 war were, in any case, soon scotched by Arab leaders. Having suffered a battlefield humiliation far worse than 1948, they were more determined than ever to reject a political compromise. At an Arab summit held in Khartoum two months after the war, they made their rejection official. They formally adopted a platform of 'three no's'—no to recognition of Israel, no to negotiations, no to peace with Israel.

The Rise of an Independent Palestinian Voice

But while it was not widely recognised at the time, the most far-reaching effect of the war in the Arab world would be to destroy the ability of Nasser, or any other Arab president or monarch, credibly to speak any longer on behalf of the Palestinians. An Egyptian-born Palestinian nationalist named Yasser Arafat and a tight band of comrades had in the late Fifties formed a new Palestinian group called al-Fatah. Within months of the Six-Day War, Arafat began to emerge as the voice of a new, militant and independent brand of Palestinian nationalism. By 1969, he—not Nasser's Shukeiri—was head of the PLO.

Israel was slow to recognise, or at least accept, the implications. It was not until more than a decade after the Six-Day War that Israel made serious attempts to negotiate a peaceful resolution of the core problem it created—the future of the West Bank and Jerusalem—with the local Palestinian Arabs who lived there rather than through Jordan or Egypt. It would be a further two decades before any direct talks with Arafat or the PLO.

The years since have been blighted by diplomatic failure, terrible violence and suffering on both sides.

The years since have been blighted by diplomatic failure, terrible violence and suffering on both sides. But neither side doubts any longer that the only workable alternative is a directly negotiated agreement, however elusive, on the future of the ancient towns and olive hilltops of the West Bank, of Jerusalem and of the Israelis and Palestinians who live there. In short, no one doubts that Middle East peace depends on resolving the decades-long repercussions of those six days of war.

VIEWPOINT 7

The Borders Established by the 1967 War Remain at the Center of Middle East Conflict

Sheera Frenkel

In May 2011, US president Barack Obama made a speech suggesting that, as a key point in on-again, off-again Israeli-Palestinian peace negotiations, Israel might consider returning to the borders it had before the 1967 war. In the following viewpoint, Sheera Frenkel writes how, despite their outward rejection of the idea, Israeli officials were pleased with the US stance because it suggested nothing new about the borders while rejecting standing plans among Palestinian leadership organizations calling for recognition of a Palestinian state. Frenkel is a journalist who reports on the Middle East for organizations such as National Public Radio and the *Christian Science Monitor.*

SOURCE. Sheera Frenkel, "Israel's '67 Borders Have Long Been at Root of Peace Debate," *McClatchy Business News* online, May 20, 2011. http://mcclatchydc.com.

Despite the Israeli government's distress over President Barack Obama's address Thursday [May 19, 2011] on Middle East issues, veterans of Israeli-Palestinian peace talks say there was little new in what the president proposed—and little chance that Israel would be forced into an agreement it found intolerable.

> Columnist Aluf Benn, writing in the Israeli newspaper *Haaretz*, even called Obama's speech a 'major diplomatic victory for Israel.'

Even Obama's invocation of Israel's 1967 borders as the starting point for a peace settlement was hardly change, despite statements from officials in the government of Prime Minister Benjamin Netanyahu. President Bill Clinton made essentially the same suggestion in 2000 and President George W. Bush acknowledged as much in a 2004 letter to then-Israeli Prime Minister Ariel Sharon.

"Netanyahu, and every other official, knows that '67 will be the basis for borders," said an Israeli official in Jerusalem who spoke only on the condition of anonymity because of the sensitivity of the issue. "It is all posturing so that they can get what they want out of their friends in Washington [the US government]."

Columnist Aluf Benn, writing in the Israeli newspaper *Haaretz*, even called Obama's speech a "major diplomatic victory for Israel."

"Netanyahu could not have asked for more," Benn wrote. "Obama outright rejects Palestinian President Mahmoud Abbas' recognition campaign, as well as the Palestinian reconciliation agreement," a reference to the recently signed unity pact between the rival Fatah and Hamas Palestinian factions.

Still, the 1967 border issue rankled. Netanyahu raised it again as he sat next to Obama Friday in the White House, flatly rejecting the president's suggestion that peace talks should start with those borders.

"It cannot go back to the 1967 lines. These lines are indefensible," Netanyahu said, leaning forward in his chair, repeating a decades-old Israeli complaint that its original borders created a country so narrow at one point that it could easily be overrun.

More accurately, the 1967 border—which roughly defines the West Bank and Gaza as a future Palestinian state—should be called the 1949 Armistice Line, since it was drawn by the United Nations based on the positions Israeli and Arab forces held when they stopped fighting in 1949.

Contentious Borders

Those lines, for example, split Jerusalem between a western portion, held by the Israelis, and an eastern, Arab side.

The 1967 Six Day War saw Israel capture East Jerusalem and the West Bank from Jordan, the Golan Heights from Syria, and Gaza and the Sinai Peninsula from Egypt, largely ending Israeli worries about its indefensible borders. Israel returned the Sinai as part of its 1979 peace agreement with Egypt, dismantling settlements there, a course it also followed in 2005 when it withdrew from Gaza.

What to do about the West Bank and East Jerusalem is a more difficult problem, however. More than 500,000 Jewish settlers live in what had been East Jerusalem and the West Bank. Most of them inhabit large settlement areas that are really suburbs of the major cities of Jerusalem and Tel Aviv, and Israeli officials have argued consistently that they'll remain part of a greater Israel.

Clinton's 2000 plan would have used the 1967 boundaries as a foundation for a peace agreement. The plan would have allowed Israel to remain in control of about 80 percent of the settlers outside the armistice line but would have required the country to turn over some pre-1967 Israeli territory to Palestinian control in return.

The Camp David Accords

Some of the issues that remained unsettled after the Six-Day War were finally addressed when Egyptian president Anwar Sadat, Israeli prime minister Menachem Begin, and US president Jimmy Carter concluded the Camp David Accords in 1978. The Accords also laid the groundwork for the first major peace treaty between Israel and an Arab state since the founding of Israel in 1948.

After being elected president in 1976, Jimmy Carter made it foreign policy priority to try to bring peace to the Middle East, using a wide variety of approaches to leaders of the nation-states involved as well as the Palestine Liberation Organization (PLO). Arab leaders were hesitant to meet with one another and the Israelis in an international peace conference, but Sadat and Begin were both open to joint Egyptian-Israeli talks. Although the two did not get along that well personally, a way forward had already been introduced when, in 1977, Sadat was invited to speak before the Israel Knesset, or parliament. Not long after, Israeli journalists were invited to Cairo, the Egyptian capital.

With progress on a peace process already underway, and with Carter open to a two-country approach rather than multilateral talks, Sadat and Begin met at Camp David, Maryland, in September 1978. Camp David, a presidential retreat, is in a fairly isolated area, making it possible for talks to take place without much outside interference or distractions. Although the negotiations were tense and halting, they finally resulted in two major agreements. One, a "Framework for the Conclusion of a Peace Treaty Between Egypt and Israel," provided for the return of the Sinai Peninsula, taken in the Six-Day War by Israel, to Egypt. The Egyptians, for their part, guaranteed Israel access to the Red Sea and the Suez Canal and began formal diplomatic relations with Israel. The second agreement, "A Framework for Peace in the Middle East," contained recognition by Israel of the legitimate rights of the Palestinian people but did little to guarantee their autonomy. It did, however, provide for the end of Israel's military government in the West Bank and Gaza Strip, which had held sway since 1967.

The government that ruled Israel at the time tentatively agreed, but after a right-wing government took control in 2001, the negotiations stopped. In 2004, President Bush acknowledged that the "1949 Armistice Line" had been the point of departure for peace talks, but

Egyptian president Anwar Sadat, US president Jimmy Carter, and Israeli prime minister Menachem Begin (from left) join hands in the White House after signing the Camp David Accords on September 18, 1978. (© David Hume Kennerly/Getty Images.)

The Camp David Accords did not settle the problem of Palestinian refugees or address territorial issues outside the Sinai such as in the West Bank or East Jerusalem. But they are considered a landmark in Arab-Israeli relations because, for the first time, the Arab world's major military power made it clear that it was ready to live and negotiate with its Israeli neighbor. Sadat and Begin received the Nobel Peace Prize for their efforts in building the Accords.

said it wasn't practical to expect Israel to return to those borders.

That Obama's effort to essentially revisit Clinton's plan drew such official Israeli anger is in part due to the continued rightward drift of Israeli politics since Clinton first pushed his plan, and a longing for the days when Bush and the Republicans were in office.

Successive polls conducted in Israel show that each year the public becomes less inclined to withdraw from the major settlement blocs, and more apathetic to the peace talks. The most recent survey, taken just days ago by Danny Danon, a right-wing lawmaker from Netanyahu's Likud Party, found that 54 percent of Israelis support the settlements.

> Polls conducted in Israel show that each year the public becomes . . . more apathetic to the peace talks.

Changing Politics

Palestinians, meanwhile, have become entrenched in internal political debate. At the start of this month, Palestinian leaders announced that they were forming a unity government between the long-feuding Fatah and Hamas parties.

The gulf between Fatah, which controls the West Bank, and the militant Islamist group Hamas, which violently seized control of Gaza, remains prominent, however.

In response to Obama's speech, Abbas' Fatah Party adopted a "wait and see" approach, expressing anger that Obama wouldn't support the Palestinians' planned bid for statehood when the United Nations General Assembly meets in September, but seeming otherwise unperturbed by what he'd said.

Hamas, however, slammed the speech as a "gift" to Israel. In harsh terms, Hamas spokesman Sami Abu Zuhri said that Obama had betrayed the Palestinians and made it impossible for negotiations to continue.

That reaction is one reason Netanyahu's government probably has little cause to worry about Obama's proposal, Benn noted in his column. The speech also outlined positions on other peace-related issues that essentially adopt the Israeli views.

"Netanyahu has nothing to worry about," Benn wrote. "There is no chance the Palestinian leadership will agree to return to negotiations under these principles."

CHAPTER 2

Controversies and Perspectives on the Arab-Israeli Six-Day War

VIEWPOINT 1

Israel's "Preemptive" Attack Was Justified

David Meir-Levi

In the following viewpoint, David Meir-Levi examines whether Israel was justified in firing the first shots in the Arab-Israeli Six-Day War. Meir-Levi argues that Israel was justified in attacking Egypt's forces first because Egypt in particular had already committed a number of actions that might reasonably be considered "acts of war" before any shots were fired. These included a massive military buildup, the expulsion of a United Nations force from the Sinai Peninsula, and blocking the Straits of Tiran. Amidst Arab hostility, Meir-Levi claims, Israel had the full right to launch an attack in its own defense even though its leaders hoped to avoid war. Meir-Levi is a historian who has taught at Hebrew University in Jerusalem as well as numerous universities in the San Francisco Bay area. He is the director of education and research at the Israel Peace Initiative.

Photo on previous page: A Jewish settlement is built in the Judean desert outside Jerusalem in 1999, on land annexed by Israel following the expansion of its boundaries after the Six-Day War. Settlements such as this one continue to be a source of friction in the area. (© **Greg Marinovich/Getty Images.**)

SOURCE. David Meir-Levi, "The Six-Day War: Israel's Defensive Pre-Emptive Strike," SixDayWar.co.uk, 2007.

By late 1949, Israel's willingness to accept the UN partition plan, willingness to establish peace with its neighbors, and willingness to repatriate refugees were all for naught. The Arab world, and especially the five 'confrontation states' (Egypt, Lebanon, Syria, Jordan, and Iraq) insisted that although they had lost 'round one'; there would be another, and if need be, another, and another, until the Zionist entity [Israel] was destroyed.

A Force to Be Reckoned With

So Israel set about building itself into a 20th century, democratic, technologically advanced Western state with a strong army. It absorbed more than 800,000 Jewish refugees who were forcibly expelled, penniless, from their ancestral habitations in Arab countries. It focused on developing its economy, creating an infrastructure that rivaled western states; establishing 5 world-class universities; and extending a broad network of social services to all of its citizenry, Jewish, Christian, and Moslem. As the population swelled, settlements in the Negev and Galilee grew in size and number. The port of Eilat at Israel's southernmost tip opened trade via the Red Sea with the Far East.

Terrorists perpetrated almost 9,000 attacks against Israel between 1949 and 1956, concentrating primarily on civilian targets.

But the Arab states were not joking when they promised 'round 2'. Unable as yet to mount another hot war, Egypt perpetrated a legal act of war (*casus belli*) by closing the Straits of Tiran, thus denying Israel any access to the Far East from Eilat. Egypt also supported the *fedayyin* ('redeemers', 'freedom fighters'), a terrorist movement in the Arab refugee camps of the Gaza strip. These terrorists perpetrated almost 9,000 attacks against Israel between 1949 and 1956, concentrating primarily on civilian targets. Hundreds of Israelis died, and thousands were injured. Israel's policy was to retaliate by mounting 'pin point' attacks against Egypt's military emplacements, rather than against the refugee camps in which the terrorists hid. Without actually adumbrating it, Israel pre-saged President [George W.] Bush's doctrine of 9/11/01: any country that harbors and abets terrorism is itself a terrorist country and thus a legitimate target in the war against terrorism. By attacking military targets (and avoiding countless civilian deaths), Israel tried to force the Egyptian government to dismantle the terrorist *fedayyin*. It didn't work.

In 1956, France and England induced Israel to join them in a war against Egypt. These two European powers wanted control of the Suez Canal; and they had their own foreign policy reasons for desiring the overthrow of Egyptian President [Gamal Abdel] Nasser. Israel was to handle the ground war, and thus end the *fedayyin* threat, while England and France would offer air support. Israel's Suez war was a brilliant military success. The whole of the Sinai [Peninsula] was captured in a few days. But under pressure from US President [Dwight] Eisenhower, France and England withdrew their air support. Due to foreign policy and Cold War considerations, Eisenhower and the USSR [Union of Soviet Socialist Republics] threatened Israel with an invasion unless it withdrew from the Sinai. Within a few weeks Israel had retreated; and Sinai was unilaterally returned to Egypt, without any negotiations or peace agreements. But Nasser did agree to have a UN peace keeping force in the Sinai, to keep the Straits of Tiran open, and to refrain from any military build-up at Israel's western border. It took less than ten years for this arrangement to unravel.

Inter-Arab rivalries during these ten years pitted Egypt against Syria, and Egyptian military interference with domestic troubles in Yemen (including the use of poison gas against civilians) had Egypt at odds with Saudi Arabia. Soon, in the context of these tensions, a number of Arab states accused Egypt of 'hiding behind the skirts of the UN' instead of preparing for 'round 3' against Israel. As a result, Nasser began a major military build-up, with the assistance of the USSR, including the illegal construction of ground-to-ground missiles in the Sinai.

The Soviet Accusation

In April, 1967, the Soviets in the UN accused Israel of mounting a massive military build-up on the Syrian border. Israel denied the accusation and invited the USSR to send observers to verify the truth. The USSR refused. But the UN, under Secretary General U-Thant of Burma, sent a commission to investigate. It quickly ascertained that the Soviets were lying. There was no Israeli military massing at Syria's gates. The reason for the Soviet deception is a matter of speculation. Most historians assume that the USSR wanted to spark a war that they were sure the Arabs would win, thanks to the armaments that the USSR had provided them. Such an outcome would cement Soviet relationships with the Arab world and push the US onto the sidelines in the Middle East.

> Egypt engaged in illegal violation of Israel's air space with aerial spying.

The Arab states used the Soviet ploy as an opportunity to regroup for 'round 3'. First, in mid-May, Egypt, Syria and Jordan formed a mutual defense pact against Israel. Then Egypt closed the Straits of Tiran, and expelled the UN peacekeeping forces. U-Thant very surprisingly removed the UN troops within a few days, leaving the field open to Nasser and his war machine. For that, U-Thant earned the sobriquet 'bungling Burmese'. Then Egypt engaged in illegal violation of Israel's air space with aerial spying by means of fly-overs in the area of Dimona where Israel had its nuclear reactor. Finally, Egypt mobilized its troops and massed armored brigades on the Israeli border. By June 1, the stage was set for war; and Nasser began announcing to the world that it was finally time for the Zionist stain on Arab honor to be expunged with Jewish blood.

With missiles only minutes away from major Israeli cities, troops and armor and air force of hostile nations primed for attack on three separate fronts, the Straits of Tiran closed, and the Arab world clamoring for the destruction of Israel and the butchery of its Jewish inhabitants, Israel approached the UN, USA, France and UK [United Kingdom] in search of diplomatic solutions. Israel's President made a groveling speech at the UN in which he implored the Arab states, especially Egypt, to pull back from the brink of war.

It is important to understand that at this point Egypt had perpetrated six specific actions which, in international law, qualify as *casus belli*, legal justification for war.

1. Conspiring with other belligerent countries (in this case, Syria and Jordan) for a coordinated attack
2. Closing Israel's access to international waterways (the Straits of Tiran)
3. Violating the terms of the 1956 armistice by remilitarizing the Sinai
4. Expelling the UN and USA peace-keeping troops from the Sinai
5. Perpetrating illegal spy-plane fly-overs to reconnoiter Israeli sensitive areas
6. Massing troops and tanks on Israel's borders.

Israel could have legally launched a defensive war after any one of these *casus belli*. It chose, instead, to try diplomacy, which not only failed to resolve the problem, but gave Egypt and Syria time to accelerate their own preparations for invasion.

Finally, in the early morning of June 5, when Israeli intelligence indicated that Egypt was about to attack, Israel launched its preemptive strike. In doing so, it

Egyptian tanks move into the Sinai Desert to join other divisions along the Egypt-Israel border in May 1967, a few weeks before Israel launched its attack. (© **AP Images.**)

applied the [US president John F.] Kennedy doctrine developed during the Cuban Missile Crisis (1962): no state need wait until attacked before taking defensive action. The Soviet missiles in Cuba were adequate provocation for the US blockade. The Arabs' massive build-up and threats of annihilation were adequate provocation for Israel's attack.

On 6/5/1967, in a pre-dawn raid, Israeli jets destroyed almost all the fighter planes of Egypt, Syria, Jordan and Iraq, before their pilots could get them off the ground. With most of their air forces a smoldering wreck, the Arabs had lost the war almost as soon as it had begun. Arab armor without air cover was destroyed by Israeli planes; and Arab infantry without armor was no match for the Israeli land forces. In six days Israel regained the Sinai, drove the Jordan Legion from the West Bank, and took control of the Golan Heights to within artillery range of Damascus. Suddenly there was a new world order in the Middle East.

Communicating with King Hussein

Israel had done much more than is generally acknowledged to avoid this war. It struck only after working for weeks under threat of annihilation to exhaust all reasonable diplomatic channels, and after begging the Arab states to honor their cease-fire agreements. But even more compelling, unnoticed by many but thoroughly documented in diplomatic archives, is the communication between the Israeli government and King Hussein of Jordan. On Tuesday, June 5, several hours *after* the Jordan Legion had begun its bombardment of Jerusalem and Petakh Tikvah, Israel sent a message via the Rumanian Embassy to King Hussein. The message was short and clear: stop the bombardment now and we will not invade the West Bank.

But King Hussein had already received a phone call from Nasser. This call was monitored by the Israeli Secret Service. Even though he knew that his air force was in ruins, Nasser told Hussein that Egyptian planes were over Tel Aviv and his armor was advancing on Israeli positions. Hussein believed him, and disregarded Israel's plea. Had Hussein listened to Israel, the West Bank would still be in Jordanian hands. Instead he sent his troops in to the Israeli section of Jerusalem. Only *after* its territorial integrity in Jerusalem was violated did Israel mount an assault on the Jordanian West Bank.

A few days after the UN cease fire of 6/11/67, Abba Eban, Israel's representative at the UN, made his famous speech. He held out the olive branch to the Arab world, inviting Arab states to join Israel at the peace table, and informing them in unequivocal language that everything but Jerusalem was negotiable. Territories taken in the war could be returned in exchange for formal recognition, bi-lateral negotiations, and peace.

Israel wanted peace. Israel offered land in exchange for peace. As Lord Caradon, the UK representative at the UN, noted with considerable surprise after Abba Eban's speech, never in the history of warfare did the victor sue for peace—and the vanquish refused.

> The world knew that the Arabs were the aggressors.

Twice within a few weeks of the war's end, the USSR and the Arab Bloc floated motions in the UN General Assembly declaring that Israel was the aggressor. Both motions were roundly defeated. At that time, the world knew that the Arabs were the aggressors, and that Israel, victim of aggression, had sued for peace both before the war and after their amazing victory.

Unable to brand Israel the aggressor, and in disarray following Israel's public request for peace and reconciliation, the Arab world faced what for it was a difficult choice. Recognize Israel, negotiate for the return of conquered territories, and make peace . . . or not.

Rather than respond to Israel's invitation, the Arab states met in Khartoum, Sudan, for a conference in August 1967. They unanimously decided in favor of the now famous three Khartoum 'NO's': No recognition, No negotiation, No peace. This was only round 3. The Arab world could suffer many more defeats before its ultimate victory. Israel could suffer only one defeat. Better that Israel hold on to the territories taken in the war. Better that the refugees continue languishing in their squalor and misery. Better that the Arab states re-arm for round 4 . . . than to recognize Israel's right to exist or negotiate toward a peaceful settlement of the conflict.

With the Khartoum 'NO's', the Arab world forced Israel to unwillingly assume control over the approximately million Arabs living in the West Bank, Golan Heights, Sinai and Gaza Strip.

VIEWPOINT 2

Israel Did Not Need to Attack in Order to Forestall an Egyptian Strike

Jeremy R. Hammond

In the following viewpoint, Jeremy R. Hammond argues that Israel's fears of an attack from Egypt were unfounded. Hammond claims that there was little reason, despite Egyptian bluster, to believe an attack on Israel was imminent. Therefore the preemptive attack that Israel mounted was unnecessary. Hammond is the editor of *Foreign Policy Journal* and winner of the Project Censored 2010 Award for Outstanding Investigative Journalism.

SOURCE. Jeremy R. Hammond, "Israel's Attack on Egypt in June '67 Was Not 'Preemptive'," *Foreign Policy Journal* online, July 4, 2010. http://foreignpolicyjournal.com.

It is often claimed that Israel's attack on Egypt that began the June 1967 "Six Day War" was a "preemptive" one. Implicit in that description is the notion that Israel was under imminent threat of an attack from Egypt. Yet this historical interpretation of the war is not sustained by the documentary record.

The President of Egypt, then known as the United Arab Republic (UAR), Gamal Abdel Nasser, later conveyed to U.S. President Lyndon Johnson that his troop buildup in the Sinai Peninsula prior to the war had been to defend against a feared Israeli attack.

In a meeting with Nasser, Johnson's special envoy to the UAR, Robert B. Anderson, expressed U.S. puzzlement over why he had massed troops in the Sinai, to which Nasser replied, "Whether you believe it or not, we were in fear of an attack from Israel. We had been informed that the Israelis were massing troops on the Syrian border with the idea of first attacking Syria, there they did not expect to meet great resistance, and then commence their attack on the UAR."

Anderson then told Nasser "that it was unfortunate the UAR had believed such reports, which were simply not in accordance with the facts," to which Nasser responded that his information had come from reliable sources (presumably referring to intelligence information passed along by the USSR [Union of Soviet Socialist Republics]).

Nasser added that "your own State Department called in my Ambassador to the U.S. in April or May and warned him that there were rumors that there might be a conflict between Israel and the UAR."

U.S. Judgments

U.S. intelligence had indeed foreseen the coming war. "The CIA was right about the timing, duration, and outcome of the war," notes David S. Robarge in an article available on the CIA's website.

On May 23, Director of Central Intelligence Richard Helms presented Johnson with the CIA's assessment that Israel could "defend successfully against simultaneous Arab attacks on all fronts . . . or hold on any three fronts while mounting successfully a major offensive on the fourth."

In an document entitled "Military Capabilities of Israel and the Arab States," the CIA assessed that "Israel could almost certainly attain air supremacy over the Sinai Peninsula in less than 24 hours after taking the initiative or in two or three days if the UAR struck first."

Additionally, the CIA assessed that Nasser's military presence in the Sinai was defensive, stating that "Armored striking forces could breach the UAR's double *defense line* in the Sinai in three to four days and drive the Egyptians west of the Suez Canal in seven to nine days. Israel could contain any attacks by Syria or Jordan during this period" (emphasis added).

Although the Arabs had numerical superiority in terms of military hardware, "Nonetheless, the IDF [Israeli Defense Forces] maintain qualitative superiority over the Arab armed forces in almost all aspects of combat operations."

Johnson himself told the Israeli Foreign Minister, Abba Eban, "All of our intelligence people are unanimous that if the UAR attacks, you will whip hell out of them."

Israel meanwhile claimed that it was "badly outgunned," apparently presuming, Robarge writes, "that Washington accorded its analyses such special import [so] that US leaders would listen to its judgments on Arab-Israeli issues over those of their own intelligence services."

Yet "Helms had the Office of National Estimates (ONE) prepare an appraisal of the Mossad [the Israeli intelligence service] assessment," which stated: "We do not believe" that the Israeli claim of being the underdog "was a serious estimate of the sort they would submit to their own high officials."

Neither U.S. nor Israeli intelligence assessed that there was any kind of serious threat of an Egyptian attack. On the contrary, both considered the possibility that Nasser might strike first as being extremely slim.

Neither U.S. nor Israeli intelligence assessed that there was any kind of serious threat of an Egyptian attack.

The current Israeli Ambassador to the U.S., Michael B. Oren, acknowledged in his book *Six Days of War*, widely regarded as the definitive account of the war, that "By all reports Israel received from the Americans, and according to its own intelligence, Nasser had no interest in bloodshed."

In the Israeli view, "Nasser would have to be deranged" to attack Israel first, and war "could only come about if Nasser felt he had complete military superiority over the IDF, if Israel were caught up in a domestic crisis, and, most crucially, was isolated internationally—a most unlikely confluence."

Israel Attacks First

Four days before Israel's attack on Egypt, Helms met with a senior Israeli official who expressed Israel's intent to go to war, and that the only reason it hadn't already struck was because of efforts by the Johnson administration to restrain both sides to prevent a violent conflict.

"Helms interpreted the remarks as suggesting that Israel would attack very soon," writes Robarge. He reported to Johnson "that Israel probably would start a war within a few days."

"Helms was awakened at 3:00 in the morning on 5 June by a call from the CIA Operations Center," which had received the report "that Israel had launched its attack" and that, contrary to Israel's claims that Egypt had been the aggressor, Israel had fired first.

Yitzhak Rabin, who would later become Prime Minister, told *Le Monde* the year following the '67 war, "I do

The USS *Liberty* Incident

During the Six-Day War, Israeli fighter planes and torpedo boats attacked the USS *Liberty,* a US naval vessel. Thirty-four Americans were killed in the attack and 170 were wounded, while the ship itself was heavily damaged. The reasons behind the attack, as well as Israel's explanations for it later, remain controversial.

The United States was officially neutral during the Six-Day War, despite the claims of some Arab officials that the United States supported Israel. Nevertheless, in order to remain well-informed about the gathering conflict, the *Liberty* was dispatched to the Eastern Mediterranean in order to gather intelligence, the task it was designed and equipped to do. On the day the attack took place, June 8, 1967, the ship was positioned approximately twenty-eight miles off of the Egyptian coast, in international waters. Perhaps confusing the *Liberty* for an Egyptian destroyer, Israeli pilots were given clearance to fire upon it in the early afternoon. Soon after a small group of Israeli torpedo boats approached and, after taking a small amount of fire from a nervous and uncertain US crew, were granted permission to launch torpedoes and fire their own guns at the *Liberty.* Israeli officials soon recognized the damaged ship as American and offered assistance, but that assistance was refused by the *Liberty*'s survivors. Still able to sail, the ship was eventually escorted to the island of Malta by other US Navy vessels, with doctors put aboard to help with the wounded.

The USS Liberty, *a US technical research ship, was damaged by Israeli aircraft and torpedo vessels in June 1967.* (**© Keystone/Hulton Archive/Getty Images.**)

Official enquiries by both the United States and Israel concluded that the attacks were the result of Israeli officers mistaking the identity of the ship, and therefore they were not intentional. Instead, the fate of the *Liberty* must be understood as one of the mistakes that often happen in warfare. Some of the ship's survivors, however, as well as some outside investigators, reject any claim that the attacks were a mistake. They argue that the *Liberty* was clearly identifiable as a US ship, flying the US flag on a clear day. While the controversy remains open, Israel ultimately agreed to pay millions of dollars in compensation to the families of those killed as well as those who were wounded.

not think Nasser wanted war. The two divisions he sent to the Sinai would not have been sufficient to launch an offensive war. He knew it and we knew it."

Israeli Prime Minister Menachem Begin acknowledged in a speech in 1982 that its war on Egypt in 1956 was a war of "choice" and that, "In June 1967 we again had a choice. The Egyptian army concentrations in the Sinai approaches do not prove that Nasser was really about to attack us. We must be honest with ourselves. We decided to attack him."

Despite its total lack of sustainability from the documentary record, and despite such admissions from top Israeli officials, it is virtually obligatory for commentators in contemporary mainstream accounts of the '67 war to describe Israel's attack on Egypt as "preemptive."

VIEWPOINT 3

The Six-Day War Resulted from Miscommunication and Misdirection

Michael Oren

In the following viewpoint, Michael Oren reports on the causes of the Arab-Israeli Six-Day War. Newly available documents suggest that Egypt was hesitant to start a war, and other Arab nations, notably Jordan, were trying to find ways to live peacefully with Israel. The documents also suggest that Israel's leaders were not intent upon a major operation in order to expand their territory but instead planned at most for a limited operation to minimize any Egyptian threat. This new research makes it more difficult to argue either that the Arab states planned to attack Israel or, alternatively, that Israel wanted to use a preemptive war to expand its borders. However, Oren asserts, the atmosphere of the Middle East was

---

SOURCE. Michael Oren, "The Revelations of 1967: New Research on the Six Day War and Its Lessons for the Contemporary Middle East," *Israel Studies*, Summer 2005, pp. 2–10. http://muse.jhu.edu.

so tense that it took only relatively small events to increase the chance of a larger war. Oren is the author of *Six Days of War* as well as many articles on the 1967 conflict. In 2009 he became Israel's ambassador to the United States.

Since that period (May, June 1967), every major event, every milestone in the Arab-Israeli conflict—the War of Attrition [1969–1970], the Yom Kippur War [1973], the Lebanon War [1982], the whole peace process, the question of Israeli settlements in the territories, the status of Jerusalem—all of these events have been the direct outcome of 6 days of intense fighting 37 years ago. There does not seem to be another example in history of an event that was so short and so limited geographically that has had such profound, long-term regional, and indeed global, ramifications. It seems safe to say that, for statesmen and military leaders, both in the Middle East and beyond, the Six Day War never really ended. For historians, it is only just beginning.

New Documents and Reports

It is only just beginning thanks to the declassification of tens of thousands of formerly top-secret documents in archives across North America, in Great Britain, in Israel, and even in the former Soviet Union, and the publication in Arab countries, Jordan in particular, and in England, of memoirs of former decision-makers and military commanders. These new sources provide us with unprecedented insights into the decision-making process before, during, and immediately after the war. They supply us with very poignant portraits of the colorful figures that made those decisions—leaders such as Moshe Dayan, Yitzhak Rabin, King Hussein of Jordan, and President [Gamal Abdel] Nasser of Egypt.

Together a picture emerges of a region deeply submerged in a context of conflict. This conflict was occurring on many levels: on the international level in the cold war between the United States and the Soviet Union; on the regional level between the progressive and the conservative Arab regimes—bitter and often fatal rivalries; on the bilateral level, in the intractable Arab-Israeli conflict, which was a perennial source of instability throughout the region.

In such a context, little was needed to start trouble between opponents. The smallest spark sufficed to set off a regional conflagration.

When the smoke cleared, 14 Jordanians lay dead. Instantly Jordan's Palestinian majority rose up in riots.

Such a spark was ignited six months before the war, on 11 November 1966. On that day, three Israeli soldiers patrolling along the border between Israel and the West Bank (then under Jordanian control) stepped on a mine. The mine was planted by the al-Fatah organization of Yasser Arafat [later leader of the Palestine Liberation Organization], and the three Israelis were killed. Two days later, 500 Israeli paratroopers, in the largest Israeli retaliation raid since the 1956 War, crossed into the West Bank with the objective of striking into an al-Fatah stronghold in the village of al-Samu'a. But something went awry in the Israeli plan: a battalion of Jordanian soldiers that wasn't supposed to be anywhere in the vicinity all of a sudden crossed the Israelis' path and shots were exchanged. When the smoke cleared, 14 Jordanians lay dead. Instantly Jordan's Palestinian majority rose up in riots complaining that Hussein was not doing enough to defend the country—that Hussein was a traitor in league with the Zionists [Israelis] and should be violently overthrown. Hussein, whose rule was never particularly secure in Jordan, panicked. He quickly sought to deflect this criticism from himself and onto his arch-nemesis, Nasser of Egypt. Hussein started claiming that Nasser wasn't doing enough to defend the Palestinians, that Nasser was secretly in league with Israel, and that Nasser was "hiding behind the skirts" of UN peace-keeping forces that had been placed in the Sinai peninsula as a buffering force between Egypt and Israel at the end of that previous Arab-Israeli war in 1956.

Mortified, Nasser now sought an excuse to get rid of the UN forces in the Sinai. That pretext was supplied by the Soviets on May 12, 1967 when they reported to the Egyptians—we now know it was not true—that they had learned of an Israeli plan to invade Syria and to capture the Syrian capital of Damascus. Nasser quickly seized on this pretext. He sent 100 thousand troops into Sinai, 500 aircraft, a thousand battle tanks. He evicted UN forces and closed off shipping to Israel's Southern port of Eilat. From that point on, it was only a matter of time and circumstance before the Israeli government decided to react to this threat and to strike preemptively. Thus began what became the Six Day War. All this happened because of Israel's raid on the village of al-Samu'a.

Now one can learn from the recently declassified documents that the raid on al-Samu'a should never have occurred; in fact, it could have been easily prevented. To understand this, one needs to rewind to 11 November 1966. In his rhetoric, King Hussein of Jordan was as anti-Zionist as any Arab leader of his day, but secretly, Hussein had managed to reach a *modus vivendi* [peaceful understanding] with Israel. He met clandestinely with Israeli emissaries on a regular basis and had open channels to the Israelis through the American and the British Embassies. As soon as he heard about the death of the three soldiers along the border, he sat down and penned a personal letter of condolence to the Prime Minister of Israel, Levi Eshkol, in which Hussein promised to do his utmost to prevent future attacks like this.

An Unfortunate Delay

The King gave the letter of condolence to the American ambassador in Amman, who passed it on to his counterpart in Tel-Aviv, a gentleman by the name of Walworth Barbour. Barbour was an interesting man: six foot six, 300 pounds, a substantive presence, who had lived all his life with his sister. Colorful though he might have been, Babour was a beloved and seasoned diplomat, who had spent 9 years as ambassador in Israel. Hussein's letter of condolence reached Barbour's desk on the afternoon of 11 November, which was a Friday. Anybody who has ever visited Israel knows what happens in Israel on Friday afternoon: everything closes down. Barbour looked at his watch, said, "It's too late to pass on this letter, it can wait till Sunday, Monday," and he shelved it. On Sunday, Israel launched its raid on al-Samu'a.

The Six Day War broke out, not because of Israeli activism, not because of Nasser's nefariousness, but because of the procrastination of one man.

Had Israel received that letter of condolence with the imprimatur of the American Embassy, the raid would never have been mounted. And so a case can be posited that the Six Day War broke out, not because of Israeli activism, not because of Nasser's nefariousness, but because of the procrastination of one man, an American, a diplomat who waited, in deference to the Jewish Sabbath, to pass on a letter of condolence.

Now the same type of quirky twisted events prevented Egypt from launching the same type of surprise attack against Israel that Israel had mounted on 5 June, and perhaps with even equal consequences. The operation was code named in Arabic *al-Fajar,* the Dawn, and it was the brainchild of the Egyptian army's Field Marshall Abdel Hakim Amer.

Amer was quirky in his own right, but in a negative way. He was a notorious philanderer and a substance abuser. He had elevated political corruption in Egypt, which is saying something, to an entirely new art form. Amer had faired very poorly in the 1956 war; he had

The Israeli army partly destroyed the Jordanian border village of Samu in November 1966, causing an already tense situation to escalate. (© **Terence Spencer/Time & Life Pictures/Getty Images.**)

failed also in Egypt's disastrous involvement in the Yemenite civil war [1962–1970]. He was looking for some way to restore his tarnished honor and he saw this operation, the Dawn, as a means of achieving that. The operation called for a massive surprise aerial strike against all of Israel's strategic targets, airfields, refineries, bases, and power plants, to be followed up by an armored thrust through Israel's Negev Desert northward, to literally cut the Jewish State in half.

Nasser did not support the operation, but he was afraid of Amer. Amer had tremendous power within Egypt, but, more to the point, Nasser also loved him. Amer was his best friend. He wasn't just his most feared political rival; he was his dear comrade. They lived next door to one another; their family members married one another; they went on vacation together. And this combination of fear and affection prevented Nasser from standing up to Amer. Nasser would have preferred that Israel fire the first shot. He wanted to provoke Israel into firing the first shot so that Israel would be saddled with responsibility for that war. But Amer said no, that Egypt should start the war, and Nasser did not stand up to him. The result was operation Dawn, set to go off fittingly at dawn 27 May 1967.

Tense Diplomacy

Except that it did not happen. The truly interesting question is, why? Because the day before, on 25 May, Foreign Minister of Israel, Abba Eban, arrived in Washington [DC] with the goal of ascertaining from American leaders their position in the event of an outbreak of war in the Middle East. As Eban landed, he was handed an ultra-secret cable directly from Prime Minister, Levi Eshkol, which stated that Israel had learned of Egypt's intention to attack Israel within the next 48 hours to lead a war of annihilation and Eban was now to find out what the Americans intended to do about it.

Eban presented this intelligence to American leaders, to Secretary of State Dean Rusk, to Defense Secretary [Robert] McNamara, and finally to President [Lyndon] Johnson himself on the evening of 26 May in the Yellow Office of the White House. The American response to this situation was virtually uniform. Listen, the Americans said, we cannot corroborate this warning; our own intelligence sources tell us that the Egyptian deployment in Sinai remains defensive. We have no evidence that Egypt plans to attack Israel in the next 48 hours.

Eban left the White House distraught; but after he had gone, President Johnson sat with his advisors, scratched his head, turned to his advisors, and said, "What would happen if they're right and we're wrong? What if their intelligence sources are better than ours and Egypt does plan to attack? Let's hedge our bets." Johnson fired off a hotline message to his counterpart in the Kremlin,

Premier Alexei Kosygin. In that message Johnson said, "We have learned from the Israelis, and, though we can't corroborate this information, they say that the Egyptians plan to attack Israel in the next 48 hours. If that's so, you had better do your utmost to intercede with your ally and prevent that from happening because you, the Soviets, will be held responsible for starting a war in the Middle East."

The results of this message came at 2:30 in the morning, when the Soviet Ambassador in Cairo, Dmitri Podjidaev, knocked on the door of Egyptian President Gamal Abdel Nasser. Nasser came to the door in his pajamas, and Podjidaev read out a sharply worded message from Premier Kosygin: that the Russians had learned from the Americans who had learned from the Israelis that Egypt planned to launch an attack at dawn. The ambassador then gave Nasser a stern warning: "don't do it," because, if Egypt was held responsible for starting a war, the Soviet Union would not stand behind its ally. They could not support Egypt in such a situation.

Nasser panicked; he quickly convened his generals and said to them, "Friends, there's been a leak; whatever you have planned for sunrise this morning is canceled." Amer said, "Not so fast." This was Amer's big opportunity; the Dawn operation was his brainchild. He quickly called the head of Egypt's air force, Major General Sidqi Mahmoud, and he said to him, "Sidqi, how long will it take to launch the operation?" Sidqi responded, "The pilots just now are climbing into the cockpits—45 minutes."

The fate and the future of the Middle East hung in the balance. During that three-quarters of an hour, Amer consulted with his own sources in the Kremlin and they confirmed the substance of Kosygin's message to Nasser that if war broke out and Egypt started it, the Soviet Union would not back Egypt. Despondent, Amer called Sidqi back and said, "Sidqi, tell the pilots to climb down, the operation is canceled."

We know from released Israeli sources that, had the Egyptians launched that surprise aerial attack, there was little that Israel could have done to prevent it. Twice on 24 and 25 May, Egyptian MIG [airplane] fighters penetrated Israeli airspace over the Negev and photographed Israel's most strategic sight, the Dimona nuclear reactor. Israeli forces fired missiles at the jets and also sent up jets to pursue them. None of these touched the Egyptian jets; they all got away scot-free. This simply demonstrated, that, had the Egyptians launched the surprise attack, Israel was vulnerable and the Egyptians could have caused extensive damage—perhaps the same type of damage that Israel caused to Egypt when Israeli planes attacked Egypt 9 days later on 5 June.

Limited Israeli Goals

Now, that operation—which we now know as the Six Day War—was conceived by Israeli planners as a two-day war. A 48-hour surgical strike, it had only two objectives: the first was to eliminate Egypt's air force on the ground in a surprise attack; and the second, was a ground operation to neutralize the first of three Egyptian defense lines in Sinai. That's it. No taking the entire Sinai Peninsula down to the Suez Canal. No occupying the Gaza Strip. No climbing and seizing the Golan Heights. No entering the West Bank. No capturing, or liberating, however one chooses to say it, the old city of Jerusalem.

How that two-day, very limited operation snowballed into this master war that trebled Israel's size in six days is an extraordinary story, and telling it in its entirety is beyond the scope of this article.

Just one episode in that saga, however, will suffice to show the uniqueness of those events and their particular salience for today. The episode in question relates to how Israel came in control of the West Bank and ultimately East Jerusalem and the Old City with its holy sites. Israel did not want the war with Jordan. The Jordanian border was Israel's longest and most vulnerable. Israel had its hands full with Egypt, and the last thing it wanted was a war with Jordan. Before 5 June, strict orders went out from the Israeli command not to open fire on Jordan, even if Jordan opened fire on Israel. The notion was that, if Hussein has to prove his Arabness, "by firing off a few shells," Israel was going to let him do it and was not going to react. For his part, King Hussein did not want war with Israel; there is no question about that. He sought every possible way not to enter into this war, but he faced a terrible dilemma. If the Egyptians went to war and the Egyptians lost the war, and Hussein had not aided the Egyptians, then the Palestinians in Jordan in particular, and the Arab world in general, would hold King Hussein guilty of treason: his life and kingdom would not be worth much. But if Nasser went to war without Hussein and proceeded to win the war, once the Egyptian army had cut across the Negev to reach the Jordanian border it would continue on to Amman, and then Nasser would kill him for having sat out the war. It was a terrible dilemma from which the King extricated himself in an ingenious way. He decided to aggregate responsibility in general for the crisis by placing his army under direct Egyptian command. Thus, on 1 June, Egyptian General [Abdul Munim] Riad arrived in Amman to take command of the Jordanian army.

"King Hussein did not want war with Israel; there is no question about that.

Unexpected Escalation

On 5 June, Israel began its attack against Egypt. At 10:30 in the morning, Israel sent a message to the Jordanians, directly to King Hussein, in which Israel stated very clearly its intent: "you don't open fire, we don't open fire, let's just let this thing blow over. It's none of our business [to fight you]. It's between us and Egypt." But at 10:00

in the morning, Jordanian planes strafed Israeli coastal cities and Jordanian Long Tom guns, situated around the city of Jenin, began shelling the outskirts of Tel-Aviv. Then at 11:15 A.M., Jordanian guns in East Jerusalem opened fire on West Jerusalem and lobbed thousands of shells into the west of the city causing extensive damage and killing 20 people. With all of this provocation, with all of this shelling, Israel still decided not to react. Just as the orders had stated before, Israel was going to let this just go by. As far as they were concerned, Hussein was trying to prove his Arabness. The shooting was not offensive, but defensive: the King was protecting himself from Nasser's wrath by proving his pan-Arab credentials rather than engaging in a serious offensive war effort against Israel.

The [Jordanian] King was protecting himself from Nasser's wrath by proving his pan-Arab credentials rather than engaging in a serious offensive war effort against Israel.

But something strange happened. At 10:30 in the morning of 5 June, Jordanian radio announced that Jordanian soldiers had taken Government House Ridge at the southern entrance of the city. To the contemporary observer, the place looks idyllic: where Government House Ridge is today, there is a beautiful promenade with a view of the Old City. Back in 1967, however, Government House Ridge was a UN demilitarized zone, a highly strategic area because it controlled the access to all the neighborhoods in southern Jerusalem. So strategically sensitive was the location, that Israel had a secret observation point just off the ridge. When this announcement came on Jordanian radio, Israel's central command called up the outpost and ordered them to confirm it, asking the commander there if he saw any Jordanian soldiers approaching. The outpost reported no movement: everything was quiet. At 1:30 in the afternoon, however, Jordanian soldiers attacked and occupied

Government House Ridge. Whereupon Jordanian radio announced that Jordanian soldiers were then attacking Israel's enclave on Mt. Scopus in the northern part of the city. Central command in Israel called up the Mt. Scopus command post and asked the same question: were there Jordanian soldiers in sight attacking the Israeli enclave? Central Command got the same, negative response: all was quiet at Mt. Scopus.

Confusion and Miscommunication

Quickly the central command concluded that there was no coordination between Jordanian radio and Jordan's army, and that the radio was actually announcing the intentions of the Jordanian army in advance. At this point it was only fair to ask what was going on over on the Jordanian side. Why were the Jordanians doing this? The answer is in a misleading telegram that General Riad, who was commanding the Jordanian army, received from Field Marshal Amer in Cairo at 10:30 A.M. that same morning. In that fateful note, Amer reported the situation on the battlefield exactly the opposite of what it really was. He reported that 75 percent of the Israeli air force had been destroyed, that an Egyptian column had broken through the Israeli lines, had cut through the Negev, was now proceeding northward, up the spine of the West Bank, from Hebron to Bethlehem, and would soon enter southern Jerusalem. It was therefore incumbent on the Jordanian army to guard the eastern flank of this approaching column by taking Government Hill Ridge. Assuming that the Israelis would try to reinforce the city through Mt. Scopus, General Riad concluded that he also had to take Mt. Scopus.

The Israelis knew that 75 percent of their air force had not been destroyed on the ground; and they knew that there was no Egyptian column proceeding up the spine of the West Bank about to enter southern Jerusalem. But what the Israelis feared as they saw Jordanians taking Government Hill Ridge and moving toward Mt. Scopus was a recurrence of the Jordanian siege of West Jerusalem in 1948, when a hundred-thousand Jews were put under siege for months on end. Not only was the siege of Jerusalem a lingering trauma for Israel's military leaders, but the event in 1948 had started with the same two-pronged offensive in the south and in the north. Israel had to act immediately to prevent the recurrence of that siege. Central Command therefore proceeded quickly to send forces with the order to retake Government Ridge, and for paratroopers to be brought up through Sinai to link up with Mt. Scopus. The paratroopers met their Jordanian counterparts near Mt. Scopus in the fierce and bloody battle at Ammunition Hill.

Two days later, by the morning of 7 June, Israeli forces had entered the West Bank to silence the guns of Jenin, and had spread on from there, to take most of the West Bank. Meanwhile, in Jerusalem, Israeli paratroopers had effectively circled the city.

To Take East Jerusalem or Not?

At that point, the Israeli government was presented with a fateful question, the answer to which still weighs heavily on the present predicament of the region: would Israeli forces enter the Old City of Jerusalem with its holiest Jewish sites, including the Western Wall? Or would they stay out? It was really only within several hundred yards of the forward Israeli position outside the walls of the Old City. Thinking back to 1967 pictures of the paratrooper standing by the wall, one would assume that the answer would be, "Oh, there's no question here—send them into the Old City." The fact of the matter is that the Israeli government deliberated painfully, extensively, for nearly twenty-four hours whether or not to enter the Old City of Jerusalem. There was a deep fear among many Israeli ministers interestingly enough—especially among the religious ministers and then Defense Minister Moshe

Dayan—that to enter the Old City of Jerusalem, with not only its Jewish holy sites, but with its Christian holy sites, including the Holy Sepulcher, would complicate Israel's relationship with the Christian world, and could even risk the severance of diplomatic relations between Israel and the Catholic countries. It was at that fateful juncture that Moshe Dayan famously said, "I don't need that Vatican; leave it alone."

Levi Eshkol, the Prime Minister, was a warm and witty man, and a leader with a great sense of the nation's Jewish past. He was not just Israel's Prime Minister: he was truly a Jewish leader. He had had a very strict Jewish upbringing, and he desperately wanted to reunite Israel with its holy sites, to reunite the city under Israeli sovereignty; but he appreciated the diplomatic risk involved. And so it was that he opened up the cabinet meeting on the morning of 7 June with the words, "Nu, what are we going to do about King Hussein?" It was Eshkol, in the end, who devised a risky and brilliant gamble. He sent a letter to King Hussein through the British Embassy. Just one copy of it exists in the British archives. In this letter he addressed the King with the following offer: "If you, Your Majesty, expel the Egyptian commanders of your army, if you regain control of your armed forces, if you accept a cease fire unconditionally, if you begin a process of peace talks with us, we will not take the Old City of Jerusalem."

Assessed in the context of the times, this was truly an extraordinary offer: the millennial realization of the Jewish vision of returning to Zion in its most practical, physical sense was within hands' grasp; and yet Israel's Prime Minister was willing to gamble it away in return for the possibility of a peace process with Jordan. The letter went out at 8:30 in the morning; two hours passed and there was no answer. At 11:30 in the morning Israeli paratroopers broke through Lion's Gate into the Old City. Two more hours passed, until the Israeli paratroopers charged with the operation reported in the words that continue to reverberate throughout Israel and the Middle East, that "Har Habayit Biyadeynu," "The Temple Mount is in our hands."

So if the Six Day War broke out because one letter—from King Hussein to Levi Eshkol—was not delivered on time, the West Bank and ultimately Jerusalem came into Israel's possession because yet another letter was delivered—a letter from Field Marshal Amer to General Riad with false information—and still another letter from Prime Minister Eshkol to King Hussein for which an answer was never received.

What kinds of conclusions can one draw from these episodes? Rather than a product of rational decision-making, of a cogent analysis of events on the battlefield, the Six Day War transpired as a result of vicissitudes that were unpredicted, the vagaries of war chants, and often just plain dumb luck.

Israel Did Not Have Western Help During the Six-Day War

Elie Podeh

In the following viewpoint, Elie Podeh examines whether Israel enjoyed support from the United States and Great Britain during the 1967 war. He writes that many Egyptians believe that such support helped Israel win the war and these claims continue to be made, not only by propagandists, but also in school textbooks. The idea took hold even though both the US and British governments issued strong denials at the time and despite the fact that there is virtually no clear evidence of Western military or intelligence involvement in the conflict. Podeh explores the appeal of this myth of collusion and some of its possible effects. Podeh is a senior lecturer in the Department of Islam and Near Eastern Studies at Hebrew University in Jerusalem.

SOURCE. Elie Podeh, "The Lie That Won't Die: Collusion 1967," *Middle East Quarterly*, Winter 2004, pp. 51–62. http://meforum.org.

> The United States' role: Israel was not [fighting] on its own in the [1967] war. Hundreds of volunteers, pilots, and military officers with American scientific spying equipment of the most advanced type photographed the Egyptian posts for it [Israel], jammed the Egyptian defense equipment, and transmitted to it the orders of the Egyptian command.

The above quote is not a propaganda item; it is taken from an Egyptian high school history textbook published in 1999. This fictitious depiction repeats older textbooks, and is reproduced in new textbooks for lower grades. For more than thirty years, a fabricated narrative of the 1967 war has been transmitted by the Egyptian education system as a fact.

Although educated and informed Egyptians may not give credence to the collusion story, it has become part of the Egyptian and Arab collective psyche.

This narrative first appeared on the second day of the war when Egypt launched a massive propaganda campaign that also included reports of false victories. Cairo Radio and Egypt's Voice of the Arabs (Sawt al-'Arab) played key roles in this campaign. While the Egyptian authorities later repudiated most of the news transmitted during the war, the story of U.S. "collusion" with Israel became an enduring myth, perpetuated in Egyptian historical writing and textbooks even decades later. Although educated and informed Egyptians may not give credence to the collusion story, it has become part of the Egyptian and Arab collective psyche.

Most accounts of the 1967 war, including recent historiography, mention the "big lie" story in their narratives. Yet, none of these studies has explored its origins and subsequent ramifications. This article, based mainly on archival material, has four aims: first, to explore how and to what end the Egypt of [President] Gamal Abdel Nasser invented the big lie; second, to describe the U.S.-British counter-campaign and the reasons for its failure; third, to analyze the conditions facilitating the fabrication of this story and its subsequent popular acceptance; and fourth, to expose the process by which the story has turned into a living myth in Egypt and the Arab world. . . .

Egypt Alleges Western Assistance

In the early hours of June 6, 1967, Egyptian media began to spread the allegation that both the United States and Britain were taking part in Israel's preemptive attack on Egypt and Syria. According to Radio Cairo, U.S. and British aircraft carriers provided an air umbrella for Israel and played an active role in the operations. In the following hours and days, the Egyptian media constantly repeated the same argument in a variety of forms.

Thus, for example, on the afternoon of June 6, Radio Cairo reported that British Canberra bombers had taken part in air strikes against Egyptian posts in Sinai and that U.S. aircraft had left the U.S. air base in Libya for Israel. The next day, Egypt's leading newspaper, *Al-Ahram*, quoted by Radio Cairo, reported that British and U.S. pilots were flying Israeli planes under the guise of volunteers and that Israeli pilots used aerial photographs taken by U.S. spy aircraft. The Egyptian propaganda machinery then let launch a barrage of reports on the Anglo-American "aggression" with Israel.

The sustained campaign retailed the claim that the current war, much like the prior one in 1956, was the result of collusion between Israel and its Western allies. This time, it was not France but the United States that had joined Britain, and U.S. president Lyndon Johnson replaced Anthony Eden [then British foreign minister] as the main culprit. The collusion claim constituted the bulk of the Egyptian propaganda campaign conducted during and after the war. The aim of the collusion story, according to historian Michael Oren, was to secure direct

Demonstrators attack the British embassy in Tunis, Tunisia, on June 5, 1967. British and US institutions in Arab countries were targeted during the Six-Day War because they were believed to be supporting Israel in the conflict. (© **AP Images.**)

Soviet assistance to reverse an Israeli victory achieved with Western support.

The Egyptian allegation was strengthened by broadcasts from Jordan and Syria, the two other parties to the fighting. In the early morning of June 6, Radio Amman broadcast that "foreign forces . . . effectively support Israel," and that "there are three aircraft carriers close inshore from which aircraft take off to bomb our forces." The radio quoted a statement by the director of military intelligence to the effect that the radar in Ajlun, Jordan, detected three aircraft carriers located between twenty and eighty kilometers off Tel Aviv [Israel]. According to the report, a group of sixteen and later a group of twelve aircraft had flown from the carriers to the Israeli airfield at Ramat David on June 5.

Syrian broadcasts repeated the information transmitted by Cairo and Amman. Radio Damascus added that a captured Israeli pilot had admitted that seventeen British Vulcan bombers, with full equipment and pilots, had arrived in Israel ten days before the outbreak of the war. These aircraft, in addition to other bombers flying out of British bases in Cyprus, allegedly attacked Syria and Egypt on June 5. The radio further reported that at the end of May, some 3,000 British troops had arrived in Israel from Cyprus, and British aircraft carriers had moved to an Israeli port on June 6.

Arab Countries Respond

These allegations had an immediate political impact: following Egypt's lead, Syria, Iraq, Algeria, Sudan, and the Republic of Yemen severed diplomatic relations with both the United States and Britain while Lebanon recalled its ambassadors. In addition, Arab oil-producing countries announced either an oil embargo on the United States and Britain or suspended oil exports altogether. Syria, for its part, closed the pipelines crossing its territory from Iraq and Saudi Arabia. Radio Cairo and Damascus even called on the Arab workers in the Arabian Peninsula and the gulf to sabotage the oil pipelines. Abdel Nasser decided to close the Suez Canal to shipping on June 6, with the intent of damaging Western economic interests. In addition, demonstrators vandalized American and British institutions in several Arab countries.

On June 8, as doubt set in about Egyptian reports from the battlefield, the propaganda campaign around the collusion story intensified. For example, Israel's mistaken attack on the USS *Liberty*, a radio ship of the U.S. Sixth Fleet near the shores of Sinai, was paraded as proof that U.S. forces were located near the battlefield and therefore took part in the war. It was claimed that the ship was engaged in monitoring Egyptian operational messages and relaying them to Israel. . . .

The credibility of the collusion claim was dramatically strengthened when President Abdel Nasser himself referred to it in his resignation speech on June 9 [1967]:

> The enemy, whom we were expecting from the east and north, came from the west—a fact that clearly showed that facilities exceeding his own capacity and his calculated strength had been made available to him.
>
> The enemy covered in one go all military and civilian airfields in the UAR [United Arab Republic]. This means that he was relying on some force other than his own normal strength to protect his skies against any retaliation action from our side. The enemy was also leaving other Arab fronts to be tackled with outside assistance. . . .
>
> There is clear evidence of imperialist collusion with the enemy—an imperialist collusion, trying to benefit from the lesson of the open collusion of 1956. . . . What is now established is that American and British aircraft carriers were off the shores of the enemy helping his war effort. Also, British aircraft raided, in broad daylight, positions of the Syrian and Egyptian fronts, in addition to operations by a number of American aircraft reconnoitering some of our positions. . . . Indeed, it can be said without exaggeration that the enemy was operating with an air force three times stronger than his normal force.

With the cessation of hostilities, Egypt's propaganda campaign continued.

Elaborating the Myth

With the cessation of hostilities, Egypt's propaganda campaign continued. Local radio stations and Radio Cairo broadcast allegations of collusion, which also appeared in bulletins by Egyptian embassies throughout the Middle East. While Arab opinion came to regard most of the wartime information provided by Egypt as false and fabricated (e.g., alleged Egyptian-Arab victories on the battlefield and huge Israeli losses), claims of collusion gained more credence.

The Egyptian foreign ministry played an important role in disseminating Egypt's claim. A typical report, published by the Egyptian embassy in Baghdad [Iraq] on June 11, stated that the "new tripartite plot" against the Arab states was prepared in advance by the United States, Britain, and Israel and drafted during Israeli defense minister Moshe Dayan's visit to South Vietnam in June 1966. The plot included a secret shipment of U.S. and British arms to Israel and a promise by the U.S. Sixth Fleet to protect it. The statement then provided a day-by-day account of the plot, beginning on May 21 and leading to the outbreak of hostilities on June 5. To show that the war was "an Anglo-American-Israeli attack," the document repeated all the known "facts" broadcast during the war, including the report of the Jordanian radar, the "confessions" of Israeli prisoners in Damascus, and other pieces of "intelligence" about the movements of U.S.-British forces.

Even more influential was the column of [reporter] Muhammad Heikal in *Al-Ahram*. In a series of weekly articles that were simultaneously broadcast on Radio Cairo, Heikal attempted to uncover the "secrets" of the war. In eloquent language, he presented a blend of facts, documents, and interpretations that could not but win the confidence of his readers. His evidence was circumstantial at best, and in many cases he twisted events. Heikal's conclusion was clear-cut: there was a secret U.S.-Israeli collusion against Syria and Egypt. (Although Britain's role was somewhat downplayed, Heikal thought it was party to the collusion as well.) . . .

The West Replies

In spite of this pessimistic forecast, the United States and Britain put up a fight. After all, this time, in contrast to 1956, the collusion claim was a lie. Both the United

States and Britain understood the adverse potential of the Egyptian allegation.

On June 6, when the magnitude of the Egyptian propaganda campaign became clear, London and Washington [the British and US governments] issued clear denials. The British, for example, stated that,

> Her Majesty's Government are shocked by reports emanating from the Middle East . . . that planes from a British aircraft carrier have been involved in the fighting. This is a malicious fabrication. There is not a grain of truth in it. It is the policy of Her Majesty's Government to avoid taking sides in this conflict and to do everything they can to bring about a cease-fire as soon as possible.

This statement was followed by another denial by Foreign Secretary George Brown and Prime Minister Harold Wilson in the House of Commons. At the same time, Brown sent a personal letter to all Arab ambassadors in London, in which he ridiculed Cairo's allegations and indicated that the only two British aircraft carriers in the area were located at Malta and Aden. A similar letter was sent to all Arab ambassadors, except that of Egypt, which had not had diplomatic relations with Britain since December 1965. Furthermore, American and British heads of missions in the United Nations (U.N.), Arthur Goldberg and Lord Caradon, respectively, delivered strong denials at the Security Council, describing Arab allegations as a "complete lie." Letters in this spirit were also sent to the president of the Security Council. Both delegations, at U.S. initiative, offered to arrange a U.N. investigation into the charges of U.S.-British involvement in the war.

The U.S. State Department named an official, Chet Cooper, to the task of countering Arab charges. On June 7, he met with the British foreign minister in Washington to discuss ideas on how to "nail the big lie." At the meeting, Cooper suggested that once a cease-fire was in

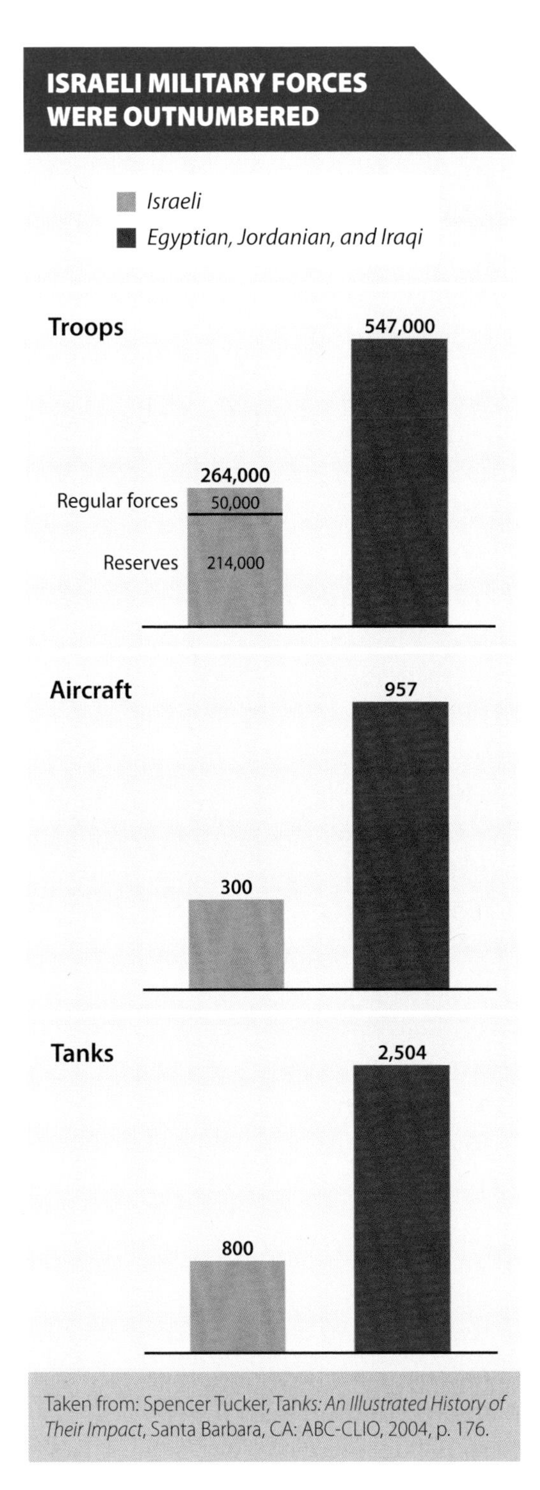

Taken from: Spencer Tucker, *Tanks: An Illustrated History of Their Impact*, Santa Barbara, CA: ABC-CLIO, 2004, p. 176.

place, an attempt should be made to "find a prominent Arab willing to expose Egyptian mendacity for what it was." He also offered to increase publicity of Egyptian use of poison gas in Yemen in order to discredit Abdel Nasser in Arab eyes. Finally, it was agreed to see if it was possible to step up transmission hours of the Arabic broadcasts of the Voice of America and the British Broadcasting Corporation (BBC).

This meeting, held only a day after Egypt's initiation of the collusion campaign, indicated the gravity with which both the United States and Britain viewed the issue. Yet, it seems that they still thought that they would be able to arrest the tide if proper measures were taken. The "big lie" was seen primarily as an alibi for Abdel Nasser for his defeat; it was not seen as a psychological mechanism for satisfying the basic needs of an entire society. Therefore, the British thought that a statement by the prime minister at that stage would "over-egg the cake." Gradually, however, Washington and London realized that the Egyptian-Arab allegations were gaining ground in the Arab world despite their efforts to refute them. Thus, Lord Caradon, the British representative at the U.N., bitterly commented on June 8: "The Arabs do not want to believe our denials."

Indeed, reports from Arab capitals indicated that both leaders and masses embraced the collusion story. Attempts by U.S. and British diplomats to refute it with logic and reason were usually brushed aside. In Baghdad, an official British démarche was received with disbelief. According to the Iraqi foreign minister, it was impossible to ignore the evidence received from Jordan (he was referring to the report of the Jordanian radar), as well as the statements of Egypt's foreign minister, Mahmud Riad, concerning the Western involvement in the war. The Iraqi response led the prescient British ambassador in Baghdad to this conclusion: "It is likely that the story of Anglo-American intervention in the hostilities . . . will become a myth."

Other Arab capitals responded similarly. Even longtime allies of the West, such as the governments of Jordan, Kuwait, Lebanon, and Saudi Arabia, seemed convinced. It is also possible that some Arab leaders did not believe in the collusion story but figured they could not swim against the tide. The Lebanese, for example, told the British that Lebanon had to demonstrate its solidarity with the Arabs, and therefore any attempt to dissuade Lebanon would not serve Western interests. Particularly hurtful was the attitude of Jordan's King Hussein, who frequently relied on Western support for his survival but now was demanding an impartial U.N. investigation on reports that British aircraft participated in the fighting.

With many Arab states either severing relations or announcing an oil embargo, it became clear to both the United States and Britain that the effects of the Egyptian collusion story were more severe than initially expected. Yet although the main problem lay in the realm of mass psychology, Washington and London continued playing on logic and reason. They believed that if they supplied accurate and reliable information, the Egyptian lie would be openly exposed. This line of thinking dictated the nature of their response.

On June 8, the Israel Defense Forces (IDF) made public a recording of a telephone conversation between Abdel Nasser and Hussein, monitored in Israel at 4:50 on June 6. The recording proved that the collusion idea had been concocted between the two leaders:

> A recording of a telephone conversation between Abdel Nasser and Hussein . . . proved that the collusion idea had been concocted between the two leaders.

> Abdel Nasser: Do you know that the U.S. is participating alongside Israel in the war? Should we announce this? . . . Should we say that the U.S. and Britain (are participating) or only the U.S?
>
> Hussein: The U.S. and England.
>
> Abdel Nasser: Does Britain have aircraft carriers?
>
> Hussein: (Inaudible)
>
> Abdel Nasser: Good. King Hussein will make an announcement and I will make an announcement . . . we will make sure that the Syrians (also) make an announcement that American and British aircraft are using their aircraft carriers against us.

London also attempted to refute Jordan's allegation that British aircraft had been detected by Jordan's radar. Following an investigation, the Ministry of Defense came to the conclusion that no Jordanian or any other Arab radar was capable of detecting British aircraft. These findings were delivered to Jordan. In addition, both the United States and Britain continued their diplomatic activity under the auspices of the U.N., aiming to erode the credibility of the Egyptian story.

But since most Western diplomatic activity was focused on achieving a cease-fire, the struggle against Egyptian propaganda could not command full attention in Washington and London. Only when the war ended did the United States and Britain tackle the issue more resolutely. By then it was already too late: the Egyptian allegation had turned into a "fact" in the Arab world. . . .

An Appealing Lie

Why did the collusion story gain such a hold in the Arab collective psyche? Why did the Western counter-campaign, which provided data and evidence, fail to sway Arab opinion?

First, the story's frequent repetition and transmission via various communication channels (radio, press, television, diplomacy, and later the education system and historiography) made the story seem truthful. A foreign diplomat once remarked in a different context: "Tell a lie long enough and often enough and inevitably you start believing it." This perfectly fits the Egyptian case.

The second reason was that the ground was well prepared for the acceptance of the collusion theory. During the first half of 1967, following an anti-U.S. speech by Abdel Nasser on February 22, Heikal published a series of eight articles in *Al-Ahram*, entitled "We and the U.S." He blamed the United States for adopting a neocolonialist policy in the Middle East, involving "economic and psychological warfare, the hatching of plots and assassinations, and a basic and fundamental reliance on secret activities." The last in this series of aggressive articles was published on May 12, less than a month before the outbreak of the war.

In addition, there were indications that in late 1966 Abdel Nasser became convinced that the United States was bent on assassinating him. The successful military coup in Greece and other coups in Third World countries led him to believe that Washington had chosen him as the next target. The collusion story was seen as a natural continuation of the charges against the Johnson administration and the fulfillment of Abdel Nasser's fears.

The third reason for the absorption of the story was psychological. On June 6, there was an urgent need to explain a chaotic situation to perplexed and largely gullible masses. Not only did the story attempt to explain reality; it was conceived as truthful because it dovetailed with the Arab nationalist narrative, which interpreted history as an unfolding of successive conspiracies. In other words, there was no need to sell or market the myth to the public because it was like an old wine in a new bottle. Thus, for example, Tahsin Basheer, a perceptive Egyptian diplomat, claims that while he did not believe in conspiracy theories, "the modern Middle East started with the [1916] Sykes-Picot agreement—a huge conspiracy hatched in the British and French embassies in Cairo [which divided much of the Middle East into British and French spheres of influence]." It was only natural, therefore, that Arab thinking would associate the collusion story with previous conspiracies, some of which did actually happen.

Fourth, the collusion story satisfied the Arab need to deny the prowess of Israel. From an Arab perspective, the notion that little Israel could have defeated three Arab states was unbearable and shameful; the idea that Western involvement played the crucial role in the defeat was comforting.

This kind of thinking, however false, contained a grain of optimism—namely, that if the might of the Western superpowers could be neutralized, it would be possible to fight on a par with Israel. Such thinking may even have helped to bring the Arab states back to the battlefield only six years after the disaster of 1967.

Although both Abdel Nasser and Heikal retracted the collusion story in 1968, it continued to be fueled by others. For example, Mahmud Riad, the Egyptian foreign minister during the war, gave the myth new legs in his memoirs. He claimed that the United States played a major role in the 1967 aggression in three ways. First, it provided Israel with intelligence information on Egyptian moves. Second, President Johnson deceived Abdel Nasser by pressing him not to make the first move while giving a "green light" to Israel to strike a preemptive blow. (Riad arrived at this conclusion on the basis of his interpretation of the diplomatic contacts between Abdel Nasser and Johnson prior to the war.) Third, the vessel *Liberty* was sent to monitor and jam Egyptian communications. In describing the U.S. role, Riad used the term "perfidy" (*khida'*).

The repetition of the [collusion] story in the schoolroom did more than anything to transform it into a living myth.

But it was the education system, and especially Egyptian textbooks, that entrenched the collusion story in the Egyptian collective memory. All post-1967 history textbooks repeated the claim that Israel launched the war with the support of Britain and the United States. The narrative also established a direct link between the 1967 war and former imperialist attempts to control the Arab world, thus portraying Israel as an imperialist stooge. The repetition of this fabricated story, with only minor variations, in all history school textbooks means that all Egyptian schoolchildren have been exposed to, and indoctrinated with, the collusion story. Undoubtedly, the repetition of the story in the schoolroom did more than anything to transform it into a living myth.

VIEWPOINT 5

US Support for Israel Came After the Six-Day War

Gulf Daily News

In the following viewpoint, the *Gulf Daily News* suggests that many of the problems in relations between Arab nations and the United States come from US support for Israel, along with the related difficulty in finding a satisfactory solution to the problem of Palestinian refugees. The viewpoint notes that staunch US support for Israel began only after the 1967 Six-Day War; indeed, while the United States sent some military aid to Israel in earlier years, its overall position in the Middle East favored neutrality. In the author's view, the increase in support should have been accompanied by greater effort to reach a peaceful solution to the Palestinian problem in the decades since 1967. The *Gulf Daily News* is published in Bahrein, a small Arab state on the Persian Gulf.

SOURCE. "US Diplomacy is Biased!," *Gulf Daily News* online, June 1, 2007. http://gulf-daily-news.com.

Facing above all the need to pacify Iraq, the US government today [June 1, 2007] has been reaching out to regional Arab powers like Egypt, but is constrained by the popular view that it is an unquestioning ally of Israel.

"The (Arab) public still looks at the US and the world largely through the prism of the Arab-Israeli issue," commented Shibley Telhami, a Middle East expert at Washington's Brookings Institution.

In October 1967, four months after the Israeli victory over the armed forces of Egypt, Jordan and Syria, the US administration of president Lyndon Johnson began a massive programme of arms supplies to the Jewish state.

Declared US policy beforehand had been to stay even-handed, with an isolated Israel surrounded by hostile Arab powers and masses of Palestinian refugees clamouring to return to their pre-1948 lands.

The United States had sold a batch of missiles to Israel in 1962 but three years later, deputy defence secretary Peter Solbert wrote: "In no case, however, will the US contribute to providing one state in the area a military advantage against another." All that changed after the Six-Day War as the United States stepped in to become Israel's leading military supplier in place of France, which as a result of the conflict imposed an arms embargo on the Jewish state.

From less than $50 million before 1967, US military aid to Israel now stands at more than $3 billion a year.

The United States was motivated also by the Cold War need to counter hefty arms supplies by the Soviet Union to Egypt and Syria.

From less than $50 million before 1967, US military aid to Israel now stands at more than $3 billion a year.

On several occasions, Washington has tried to balance its military support by acting as an "honest broker" in Middle East peace efforts, notably in the 1978 Camp

David Accords between Israel and Egypt and the Oslo Accords of 1993.

But Scott Lasensky, senior researcher at the United States Institute of Peace, said: "In the most recent period, the US has been surprisingly absent from Arab-Israeli peace making."

There Is a Lack of Support for Peace

"It's shocking that 40 years have passed and yet the US and the international community as well has not put forward a specific vision for what a two-state solution could look like," he said.

During the war of June 5–June 10, 1967, Israel captured the Gaza Strip and the Sinai Peninsula from Egypt,

Demonstrators in Bahrain protest in 2010 by setting fire to the flags of Israel and the United States, countries they believe to be strongly allied. (© AP Images/Hasan Jamali.)

the West Bank and east Jerusalem from Jordan and the Golan Heights from Syria.

Israel handed Sinai back to Egypt as part of the Camp David peace treaty, but has retained the rest in defiance of a UN Security Council resolution adopted by the United States and other major powers in November 1967.

The celebrated resolution 242 called for Israeli forces to withdraw "from territories occupied in the recent conflict" and for Arab non-aggression against the Jewish state as the basis of a lasting peace.

That "land for peace" formula remains the bedrock of peace initiatives today, and still provides an opening if President George W. Bush's administration were serious about mediation, Telhami said.

In polls of Arab public opinion, the desire remains for the United States to take a decisive role in pushing the Palestinians and Israelis to a comprehensive peace deal that would encompass all regional powers.

"You can see that by far the number-one answer is brokering Arab-Israeli peace based on the 1967 borders. By far that is the issue that they see as most important (for US policy)," Telhami said.

For Palestinians, the war marked the nadir of despair since the creation of the Jewish state: they came under Israeli occupation and their dream of a state of their own seemed to slip out of reach.

"The hated enemy, who had driven the Palestinians from their homes in 1948, was now in control of their lives, lands, and property," Israeli historian Benny Morris has written.

But it also mobilised their resistance movement and propelled it onto the world stage.

"The traumatic demolition of the status quo reawakened Palestinian identity and quickened nationalist aspirations in the conquered territories and in the Arab states," Morris wrote in *Righteous Victims*.

On the international stage, the war thrust the Arab-Israeli conflict back to the forefront, placing it smack in the middle of the Cold War between the United States and Soviet Union.

The war led to Israel's only peace treaties with Arab countries: the 1979 treaty with Egypt, with the return of the Sinai, and in 1994 with Jordan after the Palestinian autonomy deal.

> The war still casts a shadow over US diplomacy.

The Arab defeat taught Egyptians an important lesson: there can be no military solution to the Arab-Israeli problem, said Emad Gad, an analyst with the Cairo-based Ahram Centre for Strategic Studies.

"We understood Israel is the biggest regional power, you cannot destroy or remove it," he said. Egypt under president Anwar Sadat took the decision to negotiate and recovered its territories.

But the war also planted the seeds of the many deep-rooted problems that generations of diplomats have found impossible to untangle in their search for peace—from the Jewish settler movement to sovereignty over the Holy City [Jerusalem].

The war still casts a shadow over US diplomacy, with Washington struggling to navigate between its traditional staunch support for Israel and desire to build bridges to the Arab world.

It has also defied decades-old UN resolutions 242 and 338 which laid down the land-for-peace principles which have yet to be implemented with the Palestinians or the Syrians.

"It is scandalous the occupation has persisted since 1967. This conflict should have been resolved long ago, and its continuation is an indictment of all involved," from the warring parties to the big powers, said *The Economist*.

VIEWPOINT 6

Israel Needs to Keep the Post-1967 Borders for the Sake of National Defense

Dore Gold

In the following viewpoint, Dore Gold examines Israel's post-1967 borders in the West Bank and Jerusalem in the context of continued negotiations over the creation of a separate Palestinian state. Using as his starting point US president Barack Obama's suggestion in 2011 that the borders be part of any negotiation, Gold addresses the controversial issue of land swaps. This is the proposal that Israel cede some of its territory to the Palestinians in exchange for the West Bank and East Jerusalem. Gold argues that Israel needs to hold on to the West Bank because the area provides a defensible border against outside attack and land swaps of any kind are likely to be impractical. Gold has been an Israeli government adviser and has served as the nation's ambassador

SOURCE. Dore Gold, "'Land Swaps' and the 1967 Lines," *Weekly Standard* online, June 20, 2011. http://weeklystandard.com.

to the United Nations. He is president of the Jerusalem Center for Public Affairs.

When President Barack Obama first made his controversial reference to the 1967 lines as the basis for future Israeli-Palestinian negotiations on May 19, 2011, he introduced one main caveat that stuck out the idea that there would be "mutually agreed swaps" of land between the two sides. He added that both sides were entitled to "secure and recognized borders." But the inclusion of land swaps also raised many questions.

Several months after Israel captured the West Bank and Gaza in the 1967 Six Day War, the U.N. Security Council defined the territorial terms of a future peace settlement in Resolution 242, which over the decades became the cornerstone for all Arab-Israeli diplomacy. At the time, the Soviets had tried to brand Israel as the aggressor in the war and force on it a full withdrawal, but Resolution 242 made clear that Israel was not expected to withdraw from all the territories that came into its possession, meaning that Israel was not required to withdraw from 100 percent of the West Bank.

A Necessary Frontier

Given this background, [Israeli] Prime Minister Yitzhak Rabin made clear in his last Knesset [parliament] address in October 1995 that Israel would never withdraw to the 1967 lines. He stressed that Israel would have to retain control of the Jordan Valley, the great eastern, geographic barrier which provided for its security for decades since the Six Day War. He didn't say a word about land swaps. For neither Resolution 242 nor any subsequent signed agreements with the Palestinians stipulated that Israel would have to pay for any West Bank land it would retain by handing over its own sovereign land in exchange.

So where did the idea of land swaps come from? During the mid-1990s there were multiple backchannel efforts to see if it was possible to reach a final agreement between Israel and the Palestinians. The Palestinians argued that when Israel signed a peace agreement with Egypt, it agreed to withdraw from 100 percent of the Sinai Peninsula. So they asked how could PLO [Palestine Liberation Organization] chairman Yasser Arafat be given less than what Egyptian president Anwar Sadat received.

As a result, Israeli academics involved in these backchannel talks accepted the principle that the Palestinians would obtain 100 percent of the territory, just like the Egyptians, despite the language of Resolution 242, and they proposed giving Israeli land to the Palestinians as compensation for any West Bank land retained by Israel. This idea appeared in the 1995 "Beilin-Abu Mazen" paper, which was neither signed nor embraced by the Israeli or the Palestinian leaderships. Indeed, [Palestinian leader] Abu Mazen (Mahmoud Abbas) subsequently denied in May 1999 that any agreement of this sort existed.

There is a huge difference between Egypt and the Palestinians. Egypt was the first Arab state to make peace, and in recognition of that fact, Prime Minister Menachem Begin gave [Egyptian leader Anwar] Sadat all of Sinai. Moreover, the Israeli-Egyptian border had been a recognized international boundary since the time of the Ottoman Empire. The pre-1967 Israeli boundary with the West Bank was not a real international boundary; it was only an armistice line demarcating where Arab armies had been stopped when they invaded the nascent state of Israel in 1948.

In July 2000 at the Camp David Summit, the [President Bill] Clinton administration raised the land swap idea that had been proposed by Israeli academics, but neither Camp David nor the subsequent negotiating effort at Taba [a 2001 summit] succeeded. Israel's foreign minister at the time, Shlomo Ben-Ami, admitted in an interview in [Israeli newspaper] *Haaretz* on September 14, 2001: "I'm not sure that the whole idea of a land swap is feasible." In short, when the idea was actually tested in high-stakes negotiations, the land swap idea proved to be far more difficult to implement as the basis for a final agreement.

The land swap idea proved to be far more difficult to implement as the basis for a final agreement.

After the collapse of the Camp David talks, President Clinton tried to summarize Israeli and Palestinian positions and put forward a U.S. proposal that still featured the land swap. But to his credit, Clinton also stipulated: "These are my ideas. If they are not accepted, they are off the table, they go with me when I leave office." The Clinton team informed the incoming Bush administration about this point. Notably, land swaps were not part of the 2003 Roadmap for Peace or in the April 14, 2004 letter from President [George W.] Bush to [Israeli] Prime Minister Ariel Sharon.

It was Prime Minister Ehud Olmert who resurrected the land swap idea in 2008 as part of newly proposed Israeli concessions that went even further than Israel's positions at Camp David and Taba. It came up in these years in other Israeli-Palestinian contacts, as well. But Mahmoud Abbas was only willing to talk about a land swap based on 1.9 percent of the territory, which related to the size of the areas of Jewish settlement, but which did not even touch on Israel's security needs. So the land swap idea still proved to be unworkable.

What Land to Swap?

Writing in *Haaretz* on May 29, 2011, Prof. Gideon Biger, from Tel Aviv University's department of geography, warned that Israel cannot agree to a land swap greater than the equivalent of 2.5 percent of the territories since

The dispute over control of the city of Jerusalem and key religious sites like the Wailing Wall (bottom) and the Dome of the Rock (top) continues to be an obstacle to peace in the Middle East. (© **Menahem Kahana/AFP/Getty Images.**)

Israel does not have vast areas of empty land which can be transferred. Any land swap of greater size would involve areas of vital Israeli civilian and military infrastructure.

Furthermore, in the summaries of the past negotiations with Prime Minister Olmert, the Palestinians noted that they would be demanding land swaps of "comparable value"—meaning, they would not accept some remote sand dunes in exchange for high quality land near the center of Israel. In short, given the limitations on the quantity and quality of territory that Israel could conceivably offer, the land swap idea was emerging as impractical.

In Jerusalem, the old pre-1967 armistice line placed the Western Wall, the Mount of Olives, and the Old City as a whole on the Arab side of the border. From 1948 to 1967, Jews were denied access to their holy sites; some

55 synagogues and study halls were systematically destroyed, while the Old City was ethnically cleansed of all its Jewish residents. If land swaps have to be "mutually agreed," does that give the Palestinians a veto over Israeli claims beyond the 1967 line in the Old City, like the Western Wall?

The land swap question points to a deeper dilemma in U.S.-Israel relations. What is the standing of ideas from failed negotiations in the past that appear in the diplomatic record? President Obama told AIPAC [the American Israel Public Affairs Committee] on May 22 that the 1967 lines with land swaps "has long been the basis for discussions among the parties, including previous U.S. administrations." Just because an idea was discussed in the past, does that make it part of the diplomatic agenda in the future, even if the idea was never part of any legally binding, signed agreements?

In October 1986, President Ronald Reagan met with Soviet leader Mikhail Gorbachev in Reykjavik, Iceland, and made a radical proposal that both superpowers eliminate all of their ballistic missiles, in order to focus their energies on developing missile defenses alone. The idea didn't work, Reagan's proposal was not accepted, and the arms control negotiations took a totally different direction. But what if today Russian president Dmitry Medvedev asked President Obama to implement Reagan's proposals? Would the U.S. have any obligation to diplomatic ideas that did not lead to a finalized treaty?

> 'Israel must be able to defend itself—by itself—against any threat.'

Fortunately, there are other points in President Obama's recent remarks about Israeli-Palestinian negotiations that can take the parties away from the 1967 lines and assuage the Israeli side. At AIPAC, the President spoke about "the new demographic realities on the ground" which appears to take into account the large settlement blocs that Israel will eventually incorporate. Using the language of Resolution 242, Obama referred to "secure and recognized borders," and importantly added: "Israel must be able to defend itself—by itself—against any threat."

However, for Israelis, mentioning the 1967 lines without these qualifications brings back memories of an Israel that was 8 miles wide, and a time when its vulnerability turned it into a repeated target of hegemonial powers of the Middle East, that made its destruction their principle cause. Sure, Israel won the Six Day War from the 1967 lines, but it had to resort to a preemptive strike as four armies converged on its borders. No Israeli would like to live with such a short fuse again. The alternative to the 1967 lines are defensible borders, which must emerge if a viable peace is to be reached.

VIEWPOINT 7

Israel Does Not Need to Hold onto the Post-1967 Borders

Natasha Mozgovaya

Many Israelis have argued in the years since the 1967 war that Israel cannot return the West Bank to the Jordanian state or to the Palestinians on the grounds of national defense. In the following viewpoint, Natasha Mozgovaya reports that, according to former Israeli officials, including high-ranking military men, that argument is misleading. Mozgovaya maintains that all of Israel is vulnerable to such attacks whether or not the nation holds the West Bank, and Israel's defense capabilities could protect the country against a ground attack from the east. Mozgovaya is the chief US correspondent for the Israeli newspaper *Haaretz*.

SOURCE. Natasha Mozgovaya, "Former Israeli Diplomats in Washington: 1967 Borders are Defensible," *Haaretz* online, July 25, 2011. http://haaretz.com.

A group of former Israeli army officials and diplomats visited Washington [DC] Monday [July 25, 2011], claiming that a peace agreement with the Palestinians is urgent in spite of, and because of, regional turmoil, and that contrary to what Prime Minister Benjamin Netanyahu claims, the 1967 borders are, in fact, defensible.

The group visited the White House on Monday and met with the National Security Council Director for Middle East and North Africa, Steven Simon, and were to have meetings later in the evening with acting Middle East envoy David Hale and officials at the Pentagon. . . .

Among the group participants were Major General (Ret.) Natan Sharoni, a battery commander in the Sinai Campaign and a battalion commander during the Six Day War who later became Head of Planning for the IDF [Israeli Defense Forces] and Ambassador Alon Pinkas, who served as Consul General of Israel in New York.

Joining the two was Ambassador Ilan Baruch, who served with the Israeli Foreign Ministry for more than thirty years and stirred a public debate in Israel when, upon his resignation, he penned an open letter critical of Israeli government policies.

Others in the group include Colonel (Ret.) Shaul Arieli, who was Commander of the Northern Brigade in Gaza, and was responsible for the evacuation and transfer of the Gaza Strip to Palestinian control in 1994, and distinguished soldier Brigadier General (Ret.) Nehemiah Dagan.

Experienced Soldiers Speak

Major General (Ret.) Shlomo Gazit, who was head of the Assessment Department in IDF Intelligence and later became Coordinator of Israeli Government Operations in the Administered Territories, and Attorney Gilead Sher, the legal representative for the Shalit family,[1] also joined the group.

The Yom Kippur War

In October 1973, the Fourth Arab-Israeli War took place. It is also known as the Yom Kippur War because the initial attacks, carried out by an Arab alliance led by Syria and Egypt, began during the Jewish Yom Kippur holiday.

For Arab leaders, the 1973 war was an attempt to recover some of the territory they had lost to Israel as a result of the Six-Day War in 1967. Indeed, Arab nations refused to grant Israel official diplomatic recognition unless the border issues could be resolved and a solution found to the problem of Palestinian refugees. It is likely that domestic politics as well as disagreements among the Arab nations themselves also contributed to the impulse to go to war. This was especially true for Egypt's new leader Anwar Sadat, who had succeeded the late Gamal Abdel Nasser in 1970, and for Syrian leader Hafez Assad. Sadat wanted to solidify his political authority in Egypt while Assad wanted to turn Syria into a major military power. For their part, the Israelis, fearful of an attack from Egypt or Syria ever since 1967, had established fortifications in both the Sinai Peninsula and Golan Heights.

Although the Israeli government knew of the Arabs' intention to attack in October 1973, Prime Minister Golda Meir chose not to launch a preemptive assault, as her predecessors had done in 1967. Both Syria and Egypt enjoyed early successes, but they were ultimately beaten back by a better-equipped and organized Israeli Defense Forces. The conflict was ended by a ceasefire quickly engineered by the United Nations, as the major powers were concerned that the war might become a major international crisis. After all, the United States was clear in its support of Israel while the other superpower of the day, the Soviet Union, supported the Arab states.

An Israeli tank drives past wounded soldiers during the Yom Kippur War of 1973. Arabs had some early military successes in the conflict. **(© David Rubinger/Time & Life Pictures/Getty Images.)**

The agreements that ended the Yom Kippur War did not solve any territorial disputes or settle the issue of Palestinian refugees. But they are thought to have laid the groundwork for future negotiations because Arab military successes early in the conflict convinced Israel that it was not invincible on the battlefield while, for the Arabs, Israel's ultimate victory showed that there was little hope of a decisive military defeat of the Jewish state.

"We are here because we feel that we are running out of time, and there is no actual status quo," Sharoni told *Haaretz* Monday. "The dynamic is such that we must act quickly so that we don't find ourselves facing actions that cannot be corrected."

"We are here because we are concerned that the Jewish state won't remain Jewish and democratic. Thirty years from now, Jews will be one-third of the population from Jordan to the Mediterranean. And the culture that is developing in Israel these days suggests that the one-third will control the two-thirds," he said.

'To say that the strategic depth of the Jordan Valley will save Israel, that is a deception.'

The second issue that concerns the group is that no credible critics have dared to counter Prime Minister Netanyahu's claim that the 1967 borders are "indefensible."

"It has already entered the Israeli political lexicon as an axiom," Sharoni said. "We think it's misleading. The 1967 borders are defensible, we just need to define—defensible against what? It's true they are indefensible against rockets from Iran, but so is all the territory of Israel."

"They are indefensible against terror and Hezbollah rockets," he added. "But to say that the strategic depth of the Jordan Valley will save Israel, that is a deception." Sharoni said that what has traditionally constituted the "Eastern front" against Israel is now non-existent.

"Iraq doesn't have the capacity to send ground divisions against us; we have peace with Jordan, and Syria won't go to war against Israel by herself. I am sure the prime minister knows it—but he probably doesn't want to make any use of this information," Sharoni said.

Sharoni responded to a question from *Haaretz* concerning a possible threat emerging on the Eastern front ten years in the future, dismissing the supposed necessity of maintaining sovereignty over a part of the West Bank to act as a buffer zone in the event of an attack.

"Do we actually need to control the Jordan Valley to confront these threats? To move one or two IDF divisions to seize control of the Valley takes up to 36 hours. With our deterrence and mobility, there is no problem with it. If it will be a demilitarized zone—if something happens, there is enough time to get there."

"And the Palestinians need Jordan Valley to develop as a viable state, especially if they want to absorb refugees. IDF can protect any borders, it's just the question of developing the right strategy to do it," Sharoni continued.

"It is folly to measure strategic depth in another 1000 kilometers—when our entire country doesn't provide strategic depth, and frankly, I don't think any country in the world today does, against the current threats," added Sharoni.

"In 25 years, we had five wars with Egypt, from different territorial positions, and before there was a peace agreement, no borders deterred them from going to war against us," said Colonel Arieli. "Control of the territory can be replaced with advantages of other security arrangements."

"What scares us is that our current leadership has no courage and no pragmatism necessary to deal with the challenges," he added.

"I have warm sentiments for Nablus and Hebron," said Maj. Gen. (ret.) Gazit, referring to two West Bank cities that are populated almost wholly by Palestinians.

"I would love to have all of the Land of Israel. But we need to understand the difference between the defensible borders—and viable borders," said Gazit. "If the Palestinian state is not viable—we shoot ourselves in the leg."

Note

1. Gilad Shalit is an Israeli soldier who was abducted by Hamas in a cross-border raid near Gaza in 2006. He was released during a prisoner exchange in 2011.

VIEWPOINT 8

The Postwar Occupations Provided Many Benefits to Palestinians as Well as Israelis

Efraim Karsh

The end of the Six-Day War brought an immediate change in status to the more than one million Palestinian Arabs who lived in the various territories that were then added to the Israeli state. From having been citizens or protected residents of Egypt or Syria, or subjects of the Hashemite King of Jordan, these Arabs were now residents of Israel. Despite the view of many Western observers, Israel's "occupation" is not of a repressive and brutal nature, according to the Israeli scholar who wrote the following selection. He describes how Israeli occupation brought about not only social, but also economic progress for Palestine. Before Israel took over the area, Palestinian unemployment was high and life expectancy was low. All of this changed once Israel gained control of the Palestinian populations. Efraim Karsh is head of Mediterranean

---

SOURCE. Efraim Karsh, "What Occupation?," *Commentary*, July 2002.

studies at King's College London and director of the Middle East Forum, a think tank based in Philadelphia.

No term has dominated the discourse of the Palestinian-Israeli conflict more than "occupation." For decades now, hardly a day has passed without some mention in the international media of Israel's supposedly illegitimate presence on Palestinian lands. This presence is invoked to explain the origins and persistence of the conflict between the parties, to show Israel's allegedly brutal and repressive nature, and to justify the worst anti-Israel terrorist atrocities. The occupation, in short, has become a catchphrase, and like many catchphrases it means different things to different people.

For most Western observers, the term "occupation" describes Israel's control of the Gaza Strip and the West Bank, areas that it conquered during the Six-Day War of June 1967. But for many Palestinians and Arabs, the Israeli presence in these territories represents only the latest chapter in an uninterrupted story of "occupations" dating back to the very creation of Israel on "stolen" land. If you go looking for a book about Israel in the foremost Arab bookstore on London's Charing Cross Road, you will find it in the section labeled "Occupied Palestine." That this is the prevailing view not only among Arab residents of the West Bank and Gaza but among Palestinians living within Israel itself as well as elsewhere around the world is shown by the routine insistence on a Palestinian "right of return" that is meant to reverse the effects of the "1948 occupation"—i.e., the establishment of the state of Israel itself.

Palestinian intellectuals routinely blur any distinction between Israel's actions before and after 1967. Writing recently in the Israeli daily *Ha'aretz*, the prominent Palestinian cultural figure Jacques Persiqian told his

Jewish readers that today's terrorist attacks were "what you have brought upon yourselves after 54 years of systematic oppression of another people"—a historical accounting that, going back to 1948, calls into question not Israel's presence in the West Bank and Gaza but its very legitimacy as a state.

Hanan Ashrawi, the most articulate exponent of the Palestinian cause, has been even more forthright in erasing the line between post-1967 and pre-1967 "occupations." "I come to you today with a heavy heart," she told the now-infamous World Conference Against Racism in Durban last summer, "leaving behind a nation in captivity held hostage to an ongoing *naqba* [catastrophe]":

> In 1948, we became subject to a grave historical injustice manifested in a dual victimization: on the one hand, the injustice of dispossession, dispersion, and exile forcibly enacted on the population. . . . On the other hand, those who remained were subjected to the systematic oppression and brutality of an inhuman occupation that robbed them of all their rights and liberties.

This original "occupation"—that is, again, the creation and existence of the state of Israel—was later extended, in Ashrawi's narrative, as a result of the Six-Day War:

> Those of us who came under Israeli occupation in 1967 have languished in the West Bank, Jerusalem, and the Gaza Strip under a unique combination of military occupation, settler colonization, and systematic oppression. Rarely has the human mind devised such varied, diverse, and comprehensive means of wholesale brutalization and persecution.

> In 1948, no Palestinian state was invaded or destroyed to make way for the establishment of Israel.

Taken together, the charges against Israel's various "occupations" represent—and are plainly intended to be—a damning indictment of the entire Zionist enterprise. In almost every particular, they are also grossly false.

No Such Thing as Palestine History

In 1948, no Palestinian state was invaded or destroyed to make way for the establishment of Israel. From biblical times, when this territory was the state of the Jews, to its occupation by the British army at the end of World War I, Palestine had never existed as a distinct political entity but was rather part of one empire after another, from the Romans, to the Arabs, to the Ottomans. When the British arrived in 1917, the immediate loyalties of the area's inhabitants were parochial—to clan, tribe, village, town, or religious sect—and coexisted with their fealty to the Ottoman sultan-caliph as the religious and temporal head of the world Muslim community.

Under a League of Nations mandate explicitly meant to pave the way for the creation of a Jewish national home, the British established the notion of an independent Palestine for the first time and delineated its boundaries. In 1947, confronted with a determined Jewish struggle for independence, Britain returned the mandate to the League's successor, the United Nations, which in turn decided on November 29, 1947, to partition mandatory Palestine into two states: one Jewish, the other Arab.

The state of Israel was thus created by an internationally recognized act of national self-determination—an act, moreover, undertaken by an ancient people in its own homeland. In accordance with common democratic practice, the Arab population in the new state's midst was immediately recognized as a legitimate ethnic and religious minority. As for the prospective Arab state, its designated territory was slated to include, among other areas, the two regions under contest today—namely, Gaza and the West Bank (with the exception of Jerusalem, which was to be placed under international control).

As is well known, the implementation of the UN's partition plan was aborted by the effort of the Palestinians and of the surrounding Arab states to destroy the Jewish state at birth. What is less well known is that even if the Jews had lost the war, their territory would not have been handed over to the Palestinians. Rather, it would have been divided among the invading Arab forces, for the simple reason that none of the region's Arab regimes viewed the Palestinians as a distinct nation. As the eminent Arab-American historian Philip Hitti described the common Arab view to an Anglo-American commission of inquiry in 1946, "There is no such thing as Palestine in history, absolutely not."

This fact was keenly recognized by the British authorities on the eve of their departure. As one official observed in mid-December 1947, "it does not appear that Arab Palestine will be an entity, but rather that the Arab countries will each claim a portion in return for their assistance [in the war against Israel], unless [Transjordan's] King Abdullah takes rapid and firm action as soon as the British withdrawal is completed." . . .

Areas Conquered by Israel Would Not Be Given to Palestine

The British proved to be prescient. Neither Egypt nor Jordan ever allowed Palestinian self-determination in Gaza and the West Bank—which were, respectively, the parts of Palestine conquered by them during the 1948–49 war. Indeed, even UN Security Council Resolution 242, which after the Six-Day War of 1967 established the principle of "land for peace" as the cornerstone of future Arab-Israeli peace negotiations, did not envisage the creation of a Palestinian state. To the contrary: since the Palestinians were still not viewed as a distinct nation, it was assumed that any territories evacuated by Israel would be returned to their pre-1967 Arab occupiers—Gaza to Egypt, and the West Bank to Jordan. The resolution did not even mention the Palestinians by name, affirming instead the necessity "for achieving a just settlement of the refugee problem"—a clause that applied not just to the Palestinians but to the hundreds of thousands of Jews expelled from the Arab states following the 1948 war.

At this time—we are speaking of the late 1960's—Palestinian nationhood was rejected by the entire international community, including the Western democracies, the Soviet Union (the foremost supporter of radical Arabism), and the Arab world itself. "Moderate" Arab rulers like the Hashemites in Jordan viewed an independent Palestinian state as a mortal threat to their own kingdom, while the Saudis saw it as a potential source of extremism and instability. Pan-Arab nationalists were no less adamantly opposed, having their own purposes in mind for the region. . . .

Nor, for that matter, did the populace of the West Bank and Gaza regard itself as a distinct nation. The collapse and dispersion of Palestinian society following the 1948 defeat had shattered an always fragile communal fabric, and the subsequent physical separation of the various parts of the Palestinian diaspora prevented the crystallization of a national identity. Host Arab regimes actively colluded in discouraging any such sense from arising. Upon occupying the West Bank during the 1948 war, King Abdullah had moved quickly to erase all traces of corporate Palestinian identity. On April 4, 1950, the territory was formally annexed to Jordan, its residents became Jordanian citizens, and they were increasingly integrated into the kingdom's economic, political, and social structures.

For its part, the Egyptian government showed no desire to annex the Gaza Strip but had instead ruled the newly acquired area as an occupied military zone. This did not imply support of Palestinian nationalism, however, or of any sort of collective political awareness among the Palestinians. The local population was kept

As is typical in contemporary Israel, Orthodox Jews and Palestinians shop in the same market in annexed East Jerusalem in 2007. (© Awad Awad/AFP/Getty Images.)

under tight control, was denied Egyptian citizenship, and was subjected to severe restrictions on travel.

Passing into Israeli Hands

What, then, of the period after 1967, when these territories passed into the hands of Israel? Is it the case that Palestinians in the West Bank and Gaza have been the victims of the most "varied, diverse, and comprehensive means of wholesale brutalization and persecution" ever devised by the human mind?

At the very least, such a characterization would require a rather drastic downgrading of certain other well-documented 20th-century phenomena, from the slaughter of Armenians during World War I and onward through a grisly chronicle of tens upon tens of millions murdered, driven out, crushed under the heels of despots. By stark contrast, during the three decades of

Israel's control, far fewer Palestinians were killed at Jewish hands than by King Hussein of Jordan in the single month of September 1970 when, fighting off an attempt by Yasir Arafat's PLO to destroy his monarchy, he dispatched (according to the Palestinian scholar Yezid Sayigh) between 3,000 and 5,000 Palestinians, among them anywhere from 1,500 to 3,500 civilians. Similarly, the number of innocent Palestinians killed by their Kuwaiti hosts in the winter of 1991, in revenge for the PLO's support for Saddam Hussein's brutal occupation of Kuwait, far exceeds the number of Palestinian rioters and terrorists who lost their lives in the first intifada [uprising] against Israel during the late 1980's.

To present the Israeli occupation of the West Bank and Gaza as 'systematic oppression' is itself the inverse of the truth.

Such crude comparisons aside, to present the Israeli occupation of the West Bank and Gaza as "systematic oppression" is itself the inverse of the truth. It should be recalled, first of all, that this occupation did not come about as a consequence of some grand expansionist design, but rather was incidental to Israel's success against a pan-Arab attempt to destroy it. Upon the outbreak of Israeli-Egyptian hostilities on June 5, 1967, the Israeli government secretly pleaded with King Hussein of Jordan, the de-facto ruler of the West Bank, to forgo any military action; the plea was rebuffed by the Jordanian monarch, who was loathe to lose the anticipated spoils of what was to be the Arabs' "final round" with Israel.

Thus it happened that, at the end of the conflict, Israel unexpectedly found itself in control of some one million Palestinians, with no definite idea about their future status and lacking any concrete policy for their administration. In the wake of the war, the only objective adopted by then-Minister of Defense Moshe Dayan was to preserve normalcy in the territories through a mixture of economic inducements and a minimum of Israeli intervention. The idea was that the local populace would be given the freedom to administer itself as it wished, and would be able to maintain regular contact with the Arab world via the Jordan River bridges. In sharp contrast with, for example, the U.S. occupation of postwar Japan, which saw a general censorship of all Japanese media and a comprehensive revision of school curricula, Israel made no attempt to reshape Palestinian culture. It limited its oversight of the Arabic press in the territories to military and security matters, and allowed the continued use in local schools of Jordanian textbooks filled with vile anti-Semitic and anti-Israel propaganda.

At the inception of the occupation, conditions in the territories were quite dire.

Economic and Social Progress of Palestinians Under Israeli Control

Israel's restraint in this sphere—which turned out to be desperately misguided—is only part of the story. The larger part, still untold in all its detail, is of the astounding social and economic progress made by the Palestinian Arabs under Israeli "oppression." At the inception of the occupation, conditions in the territories were quite dire. Life expectancy was low; malnutrition, infectious diseases, and child mortality were rife; and the level of education was very poor. Prior to the 1967 war, fewer than 60 percent of all male adults had been employed, with unemployment among refugees running as high as 83 percent. Within a brief period after the war, Israeli occupation had led to dramatic improvements in general well-being, placing the population of the territories ahead of most of their Arab neighbors.

In the economic sphere, most of this progress was the result of access to the far larger and more advanced Israeli economy: the number of Palestinians working in Israel rose from zero in 1967 to 66,000 in 1975 and 109,000 by 1986, accounting for 35 percent of the employed population of the West Bank and 45 percent in Gaza. Close to 2,000 industrial plants, employing almost half of the work force, were established in the territories under Israeli rule.

During the 1970's, the West Bank and Gaza constituted the fourth fastest-growing economy in the world—ahead of such "wonders" as Singapore, Hong Kong, and Korea, and substantially ahead of Israel itself. Although GNP per capita grew somewhat more slowly, the rate was still high by international standards, with per-capita GNP expanding tenfold between 1968 and 1991 from $165 to $1,715 (compared with Jordan's $1,050, Egypt's $600, Turkey's $1,630, and Tunisia's $1,440). By 1999, Palestinian per-capita income was nearly double Syria's, more than four times Yemen's, and 10 percent higher than Jordan's (one of the better-off Arab states). Only the oil-rich Gulf states and Lebanon were more affluent.

Under Israeli rule, the Palestinians also made vast progress in social welfare. Perhaps most significantly, mortality rates in the West Bank and Gaza fell by more than two-thirds between 1970 and 1990, while life expectancy rose from 48 years in 1967 to 72 in 2000 (compared with an average of 68 years for all the countries of the Middle East and North Africa). Israeli medical programs reduced the infant-mortality rate of 60 per 1,000 live births in 1968 to 15 per 1,000 in 2000 (in Iraq the rate is 64, in Egypt 40, in Jordan 23, in Syria 22). And under a systematic program of inoculation, childhood diseases like polio, whooping cough, tetanus, and measles were eradicated.

No less remarkable were advances in the Palestinians' standard of living. By 1986, 92.8 percent of the population in the West Bank and Gaza had electricity around the clock, as compared to 20.5 percent in 1967; 85 percent had running water in dwellings, as compared to 16 percent in 1967; 83.5 percent had electric or gas ranges for cooking, as compared to 4 percent in 1967; and so on for refrigerators, televisions, and cars.

Finally, and perhaps most strikingly, during the two decades preceding the intifada of the late 1980's, the number of schoolchildren in the territories grew by 102 percent, and the number of classes by 99 percent, though the population itself had grown by only 28 percent. Even more dramatic was the progress in higher education. At the time of the Israeli occupation of Gaza and the West Bank, not a single university existed in these territories. By the early 1990's, there were seven such institutions, boasting some 16,500 students. Illiteracy rates dropped to 14 percent of adults over age 15, compared with 69 percent in Morocco, 61 percent in Egypt, 45 percent in Tunisia, and 44 percent in Syria.

Israel's Postwar Occupations Imposed Harsh Conditions on Palestinians

Ilan Pappe

In the following viewpoint, Ilan Pappe examines the measures the Israeli government has taken since the 1967 war to maintain control of the new territories that it occupied. These have included encouraging the building of Jewish settlements, ranging from suburbs overlooking Arab East Jerusalem to larger communities in the West Bank. According to Pappe, this has often resulted in the continued dislocation and expulsion of Arabs—a violation of international standards. Pappe suggests that the Israelis have applied their own laws inconsistently, and they have adopted practices toward Palestinian Arabs that amount to collective punishment—when a people has its rights restricted because of its ethnicity. Throughout the years since the Six-Day War, Pappe argues, the

---

SOURCE. Ilan Pappe, *A History of Modern Palestine: One Land, Two Peoples*. New York: Cambridge University Press, 2004, pp. 196–200.

Israelis have viewed the Palestinians as a subject population rather than fellow citizens. Pappe was born in Haifa, Israel, and is a veteran of the Israeli army. He is a professor at the University of Exeter in the United Kingdom.

For years Israeli leaders tended to talk about 'an enlightened occupation' when assessing the first decade of Israeli rule in the West Bank and the Gaza Strip. From its beginning, however, when 590,000 Palestinians in the West Bank and 380,000 in the Gaza Strip fell under Israeli hegemony, there was little that could be described as 'enlightened' about the harsh and brutal occupation. The first blow inflicted on the population was the Israeli expulsion policy. The pragmatic leadership of the Jewish state, although exhilarated by its sudden acquisition of the whole of ex-Mandate [post-1948] Palestine, was nonetheless nervous about absorbing such a large number of Palestinians. Expulsion was neither an alien concept nor an unfamiliar practice to the Zionist movement. Immediately after the war, the former head of military intelligence, Chaim Herzog, was appointed as governor-general, so to speak, first of Jerusalem and then of the whole West Bank. Under his administration, on 17 June 1967 Palestinian citizens living within the Jewish quarter of the Old City of Jerusalem were either evicted or offered money to leave. All were asked to sign a document relinquishing their right of return. The residents of three refugee camps north of Jericho were expelled too. A number also fled during the war and after the expulsions. In Palestinian discourse they are referred to as *nazihun* ('uprooted'), to distinguish them from the *laji'un*, the 1948 refugees. Only one expulsion attempt by Israel failed: a 1971 plan to transfer refugees from the Gaza Strip to the West Bank. A few hundred inhabitants of the Jabaliyya camp were transferred to the West Bank, but local resistance dissuaded the Israelis from further expulsions.

Palestinian demonstrators hurl stones at Israeli troops in an East Jerusalem neighborhood in 2010. More than thirty years after the Six-Day War, Palestinians continue to have violent clashes with the Israelis about their status and the country's borders. (© **AP Images/ Oded Bality.**)

Expulsion and New Settlements

Jerusalem not only saw the beginning of the Israeli expulsion policy, it was also the site of the first 'pilot project' of Jewish settlement on occupied territory. In early 1968, the Israeli authorities appropriated vast areas of East Jerusalem, a third of which were private property, and re-zoned them as new Jewish neighbourhoods. Alarmed architects and ecologists warned the municipality in vain that the hasty decision, motivated by ideology and taken without any serious environmental planning, would be disastrous. Jerusalem was thereafter encircled by several ugly suburbs, which crouched menacingly on the hills overlooking the Arab city below.

The Israeli government was still formulating its policy towards the most recent refugees. In August, it announced that it was willing to allow the repatriation of refugees who had left after 1967, but understandably these overtures were met with suspicion, and only 150 people returned. After that, the unofficial Israeli policy was not to allow refugees to return to the occupied territories. This policy became official in 1977, when Likud [a center-right political party], came to power with Menachem Begin as the prime minister. His government adhered to a Greater Israel ideology: any decrease in the number of Palestinians, or increase in the number of Jewish settlers, in the occupied territories was seen as likely to help make the dream a reality. (Many in the Labour Party also supported this stance.) Thus, the threat of expulsion and relocation was one of the many burdens imposed by the occupation on the local population. It is difficult to describe its worst aspects. While mass expulsions took place at long intervals, passive bystanders and activists alike were subjected to military harassment in the form of house searches, curfews and abusive interrogation at checkpoints on a daily basis.

Any show of opposition . . . was met with severe brutality.

'Resistance' was, in the eyes of the Israelis, very liberally defined. Any show of opposition to the occupation, such as a rally, a strike, distribution of petitions or the waving of the Palestinian flag, was met with severe brutality. The Israeli campaign against political activity began in July 1967 with the expulsion from East Jerusalem of four notables who called on the population to adopt [Indian revolutionary] Mahatma Gandhi's tactic of civil disobedience. (Many years later, when an American Palestinian, Mubarak Awad, tried to introduce a more sophisticated version of non-violent resistance he was treated by the Israelis as an arch-terrorist.) Worse was to come. Moshe Dayan, the Israeli minister of defence, was told in July 1967 of armed resistance in the West Bank town of Qalqilya, and immediately ordered, as the first act of collective punishment in a long series of such acts, the destruction of the town. Half of Qalqilya's houses were demolished in this operation.

Targeting Palestinian Resistance

Ariel Sharon, the commander in charge of the Gaza Strip, was particularly zealous in the quelling of resistance, individual or collective. Since presiding over a massacre in Qibyya in 1953, his career had been punctuated by bloody clashes with Palestinians everywhere. At first, Sharon was content to leave in charge the local notables who had run the municipal and legal systems during the Egyptian era. Thus for instance, as in the West Bank, the education system was restored to the status quo ante [as it was before], which meant Jordanian supervision in the West Bank and Egyptian supervision in the Gaza Strip. However, Sharon soon realized that he was dealing with a highly politicized refugee community, which could not easily be co-opted to this pattern of continuity. They tested his authority by questioning Israel's or Egypt's authority in the camps. Time after time, the youth, and some middle-aged men and women, took up arms, and used stones, Molotov cocktails and whatever they could find in a show of resistance against the Israeli occupation. These early attempts at revolution were soon quashed under the fire-power of tanks and heavy guns employed indiscriminately against the local civilian population. It was not until the 1987 intifada [uprising], and then the al-Aqsa intifada (*Intifadat al-Aqsa*) in the autumn of 2000, that the Israeli army resorted again to such destructive retaliation against a popular uprising.

A Special Legal Status for the Occupied Territories

The ability of the army to deal so harshly with any form of political resistance, armed or peaceful, was underwritten by the legal status Israel granted to the West Bank and the Gaza Strip. The Israeli government declared from the very onset of its occupation that these areas were 'territories under custody' in which military rule would apply. This somewhat anaemic phrase meant that in practice the people living in the territories were robbed of all basic human or civic rights. At the same time, the government did all it could to avoid being limited by international law guidelines on the administration of occupied areas; guidelines that were systematically violated by the Israelis. For that purpose, in January 1968 the Israeli minister of the interior declared that the West Bank, the Gaza Strip and the Golan Heights were not 'enemy areas'. This allowed Israel to alternate between the application of Israeli law, as in the Golan Heights, where it granted civil rights to a small community of Druzes, and the deprivation of such rights in all the other areas. The international community was not oblivious of these practices and there were objections, but the uproar subsided before it made any impact on Israeli conduct.

The legal basis for this regime was the notorious mandatory emergency regulations of 1945, which were mentioned in the previous chapter as the legal basis for the military regime imposed on the Palestinians in Israel until 1966. The Israelis now added a new regulation allowing the army to expel from anywhere in Israel and Palestine anyone suspected of being a security risk. It was used extensively, against Palestinian activists within the state of Israel as well those living in the occupied territories.

The Israelis must take sole responsibility for imposing a regime devoid of any democratic rights.

The Israeli government claimed that all it did was to continue Jordanian adherence to these regulations. This was unfounded. The Jordanians had never used these regulations, nor had the Egyptians in the Gaza

Strip. This is not to say that the Jordanians and the Egyptians had respected civic and human rights, they had not, but the Israelis must take sole responsibility for imposing a regime devoid of any democratic rights.

The Israeli military authorities used this military regime excessively in the first decade after the 1967 war. By 'excessively' I mean frequent acts of collective punishment for any gesture that was regarded as subversive or resistant to Israeli occupation. The destruction of houses, expulsion, and arrest without trial were the most common uses of the regulations. As under military rule in Israel, the formal right to vote and be elected remained, but was meaningless as it did not include the right to form independent parties. In 1972 and 1976, the Israelis allowed the population to vote in municipal elections. However, after a sweeping victory for PLO [Palestine Liberation Organization] candidates in 1976, the Likud government, coming to power in 1977, banned elections and with it deprived the local population of their remaining rights.

New Freedoms Were a Farce

From the beginning of the occupation, international jurists commented on the illegitimacy of the Israeli resolution to maintain the territories as an occupied area without adhering to the requirements sanctioned by the Geneva Convention for the treatment of such areas. Israel violated almost every clause in that convention by settling Jews there, expelling Palestinians and imposing collective punishment. The Israeli Supreme Court took upon itself the task of monitoring the legitimacy of the regime very early in the occupation. In the history of modern warfare, there is no case, apart from this one, in which a civilian judicial authority supervised military rule. This extraordinary resolution was taken in 1967 when Meir Shamgar, who went from being the military attorney-general to the government's legal adviser,

The Palestine Liberation Organization and the Palestinian Authority

After the Six-Day War, the Palestine Liberation Organization (PLO) grew to be the recognized representative of Palestinian Arab peoples, whether they were refugees of the original founding of Israel in 1948, people displaced by the 1967 conflict, the descendants of those refugees, or even Palestinians currently living in Israel.

Before the Six-Day War, the PLO had little impact and attracted little attention, but afterward it grew more militant and assertive. PLO leaders, notably Yasser Arafat, who was the face of the organization from 1969 until his death in 2004, were no longer willing to follow the lead of Egypt, Jordan, or Syria after Israel's decisive victory in the war. In addition, the war itself created many thousands of new refugees and changed the territorial calculations as Israel took possession of the West Bank, Gaza Strip, and East Jerusalem. Among other considerations, it was no longer thought possible to carve out a Palestinian state from lands held by Arab countries, as some had argued earlier. From camps in Jordan, the PLO engaged in a low-level war of attrition against Israel in 1969 and 1970, which involved attacks by fedayeen, or PLO fighters, and Israeli responses. The Jordanians eventually closed the PLO camps, while the organization's leaders operated from headquarters in Syria, Lebanon, or Tunisia. Meanwhile, militancy continued with numerous terrorist attacks in the 1970s as well as with the first intifada, or uprising, beginning in 1987. This was a broad-based protest movement in Palestinian areas that included periodic acts of violence as well as such measures as demonstrations and boycotts. By that time, the PLO had developed an elaborate leadership structure and elements of a civil government.

In 1987 PLO leaders made what amounted to a declaration of independence for a Palestinian state, a move which was seen as an official recognition of Israel, or at least an Israel with 1967's borders. Both the UN and the United States approved, with the latter beginning official diplomatic contact with the PLO. Then, in 1993, Yasser Arafat and Israeli prime minister Yitzhak Rabin concluded the Oslo Accords. This agreement effectively traded PLO recognition of Israel for the rule by a Palestinian Authority of the Gaza Strip and the city of Jericho in the West Bank. Eventually the Palestinian Authority, with Arafat as its first president, set up its headquarters in the city of Ramallah in the West Bank.

The Palestinian Authority, now known formally as the Palestinian National Authority, continues to work for the establishment of a Palestinian state. A second intifada, the emergence of vocal alternatives such as Hamas (which is linked to Islamist terrorism and governs the Gaza Strip), and Israeli concerns and hesitations lead to a troublesome future for the goal of Middle Eastern peace.

allowed Palestinians in the occupied territories to appeal to the Supreme Court. By 1988, almost 40 per cent of appeals to the Supreme Court were from Palestinians there. In practice, this allowance achieved little. Hardly any of the appeals could stand if the army asked the courts to authorize and legitimize its acts retrospectively against individuals or collectives in the name of security.

> The restrictions imposed on freedom of movement were, and still are, harsher on those seeking to leave the West Bank and the Gaza Strip.

The only respite from this predicament was, ironically, to move to East Jerusalem. In 1976, Israel, on the one hand, had annexed East Jerusalem, a part of Palestine that enjoyed a relatively open environment. On the other hand, the annexation robbed the city of its Palestinian identity, and was accompanied by the construction of illegal settlements. Many Palestinian newspapers and journals, however, moved their editorial offices to Jerusalem, hoping to be able to publish more freely, a hope not always fulfilled.

Moving to Jerusalem, or between any destinations in the occupied territories, has remained the exclusive right of Jewish settlers and those locals with special permission to do so. The restrictions imposed on freedom of movement were, and still are, harsher on those seeking to leave the West Bank and the Gaza Strip. This hardship was particularly acute in the case of Palestinian workers who were invited to join, as unskilled labourers, the booming Israeli economy around 1968. As early as November 1967, workers were reported as creeping illegally into Israel to find jobs in the orange groves. They were paid a quarter of the average Jewish salary at the time. The workers were allowed to enter Israel at dawn, but had to leave by dusk. A year later, in September 1968, the Israeli government legalized what the minister of interior called the 'import of workers, since we lack "ordinary" workers'.

CHAPTER 3

Personal Narratives

An Egyptian General Describes the Army's Strategies Against Israel

Shafik Shazly

Photo on previous page: Israeli troops mobilize against Egypt in June 1967. Civilians cheer them on from the side of the road. (© Mondadori via Getty Images.)

In the following viewpoint, a former Egyptian general recounts his experiences during the 1967 Arab-Israeli Six-Day War and the 1973 Yom Kippur War. He discusses his discovery that even though Egyptian president Gamal Abdel Nasser had expected an Israeli attack, the Egyptian planes were left lined up in airfields and were quickly destroyed by the enemy. Without their planes, Egypt never had a chance in the war, he writes. Shafik Shazly was jailed for criticizing the government after seeing his army lose two wars with Israel.

When Israel launched its surprise attack on June 5, 1967, I was meeting with all the other Sinai commanders near the Suez Canal. If they had known this, the Israelis could have wiped out our

SOURCE. Shafik Shazly, "No Match for Israel," *Newsweek*, March 15, 1999.

entire command structure with one bomb right at the beginning. As it was, when the first shells hit just before 8 A.M., not a field commander was with his troops. I rushed back to my unit, which was in a remote part of the desert near the Israeli border. Although we had lost communications, I knew the Israelis had already destroyed our Air Force simply because they ruled the skies.

> Those first two days were euphoric as we started to erase the pain of 1967.

Later we learned President [of Egypt] Gamal Abdel Nasser had expected an attack. Yet our planes were lined up on the airfields. They were sitting ducks and destroyed in the first two hours. It was our biggest mistake. Without them, we never had an opportunity to fight. My unit was the last to retreat over the Suez Canal, and after I crossed, our engineers blew the bridges. The Sinai was in Israeli hands.

Experiences of the 1973 Yom Kippur War

In 1973 I was chief of staff. I knew that because it was small, Israel couldn't bear casualties and couldn't fight a prolonged war. We had re-equipped with new arms since the 1967 humiliation. We crossed the Suez Canal on October 6, the Jewish holy day of Yom Kippur, and destroyed the supposedly impregnable Bar-Lev line. We had them on the run, as did the Syrians on the Golan Heights. Those first two days were euphoric as we started to erase the pain of 1967. My plan was to go only 15 kilometers past the Suez and then engage the Israelis in a war of attrition. If we had stayed where we were, we would have been in a good position. One or two years of war wouldn't have mattered to me, but, with 18 percent of its Jewish population mobilized, would have seriously hurt Israel.

But Anwar Sadat, who had little military experience, insisted over my protests that we move forward. He stretched our lines to 50 kilometers, taking our troops and armor out from under protection of air antiaircraft missiles. In addition, we couldn't move our few mobile missiles, the Soviet-made SAM-6s, because Moscow didn't want to risk having their latest technology fall into enemy hands. Our Air Force had yet to recover fully from 1967, so once again our troops were exposed to Israeli jets. We suffered heavy losses.

In 1967 there was no real preparation for war. In 1973 our preparations were undermined by Sadat. What is ridiculous today is that all these facts, which are well known to Israel and all over the world, are still not being told to the Egyptian people.

General Moshe Dayan Recounts the Taking of East Jerusalem

Moshe Dayan

For many Israelis, one of the great triumphs of the Six-Day War was taking parts of Jerusalem: an ancient city holy to Jews, Christians, and Muslims. It possesses a special significance for Jews, having served as the capital of the ancient kingdom of Israel, established some three thousand years ago, and as the location of the first and second temples of the Jewish faith. The only portion of those temples that remains standing is known as the Western Wall, or Wailing Wall, and the site is one of pilgrimage and remembrance for Jews. In the following viewpoint, Moshe Dayan describes how Israeli forces completed their liberation of Jerusalem in the 1967 war by occupying those areas previously under Arab control. For Dayan, the event was one of great emotional and historical significance, a completion of the reestablishment of a Jewish state. Dayan was Israel's minister of defense during the Six-Day War of 1967.

SOURCE. Moshe Dayan, *Moshe Dayan: Story of My Life*. New York: HarperCollins Publishers and the Orion Publishing Group Ltd., 1976, pp. 13–17.

It was noontime Tuesday, the second day of the Six Day War. Twenty-four hours earlier Jordanian artillery had pounded the Jewish areas of Jerusalem. [Colonel] Motta Gur's paratroop brigade had gone into action after midnight and following bitter battles throughout the hours of darkness had captured the Arab Legion fortifications on the northern outskirts of the Old City. [Major-General] Uri Ben-Ari had just signaled that his mechanized brigade had captured French Hill. Thus, the road to Mount Scopus was almost open, and Scopus, which had been an Israeli enclave in hostile Jordanian territory for nineteen years, was about to be linked to the Jewish half of Jerusalem. I decided to go there.

My helicopter landed outside the Jerusalem Convention Hall, where [overall military commander] Uzi Narkiss had established his Central Command forward headquarters. He said that fighting was still going on and we had not yet linked up with Mount Scopus. But I did not care to wait, and I pressed Uzi to start moving. He led me over to the vehicle park and stopped at a closed armored half-track. Fortunately the driver was unable to start the engine, so we set off in an open command car and jeep. With me were Chief of Operations Ezer Weizman and his deputy Gandi, and my military secretary, Yehoshua Raviv. Uzi drove and I sat next to him—a familiar pattern, for that is how we had driven from E-Tor on the Suez Gulf to Sharm el-Sheikh some ten years earlier, during the Sinai Campaign. Then, too, the road had not yet been cleared of the enemy.

We proceeded to the Pagi Quarter—the jump-off point for the paratroopers during the night—and from there, along a track which had been cleared of mines, up to the Police Training School below Ammunition Hill. The buildings were shattered and still smoking, but it was possible to get through. We stopped for a few minutes at the newly captured Ambassador Hotel to look around, particularly at the wadi which lies between Jerusalem and Scopus. We saw no Arabs. The civilians had shut themselves in their houses. They had apparently learned the lessons of 1948 and this time did not flee. I saw no reason to wait, and we pushed on to Scopus. On the way up the slope, we spotted occasional clusters of Arab Legion troops on the adjoining hills. They were no doubt survivors of the night's grim battles, and now they stood surprised and hesitant, not knowing what to do with themselves—or, fortunately, to us.

We saw no Arabs. The civilians had shut themselves in their houses.

Entering the Old City for the First Time

At the entrance gate to the Mount Scopus zone, we met the first Israeli soldiers from this outpost, and they seemed even more surprised than the Arab Legionaries had been. I asked to be taken to the observation post, and the commander, Menahem Sharfman, a Galilean from Yavniel and an old friend, took us to the roof of the National Library building. This was part of the original Hebrew University campus, and access to this center of higher learning, and to the adjoining Hadassah Hospital, had been barred by the Jordanians since 1948. From the roof we had a superb view of the city. From all sides came the sounds of artillery and light-weapons fire. In the north, Uri's 10th Brigade was fighting its way toward us, and battling in the west and south were Motta Gur's paratroopers and Eliezer Amitai's Jerusalem Brigade. Yet the Old City seemed still. Its crenellated stone walls, the Temple Mount, the mosques, the olive trees, the surrounding hills, all gave forth an air of calm, of majestic indifference to the explosive booms resounding all around them. I looked down upon this walled city in all its strength and splendor, wrapped in eternal tranquillity.

I had waited nineteen years for this moment. In 1948, when I was commander of Jerusalem, and later, when I

was chief of staff, I had cherished the hope of a liberated Jerusalem and a freed Mount Scopus. Throughout all the generations, during the two thousand years of their exile, the Jewish people had yearned for Jerusalem. It was the object of their pilgrimage, their dreams, their longings. In the previous two decades, this craving of the centuries had found expression in operational plans. Jerusalem and its environs had a place in the General Staff files, on air reconnaissance photographs, and in exercises at the sand table. But Jerusalem's permanent place was in the heart.

There are moments which bear within them solace for the sufferings of a nation, consolation for a private loss, reward for the fearless and unremitting pursuit of a noble goal. This was one of them. It was with reluctance that I turned from this view of Jerusalem and clambered down from the roof.

Twenty-four hours later, I was again at Central Command advance headquarters, but this time we drove to the Old City. It had been captured shortly before by Gur's paratroops. They had crashed through the Lions' Gate, and a few minutes later Gur signaled "The Temple Mount is ours. Repeat: The Temple Mount is ours."

As we drove, the sounds of volleys came from the northeast corner of the city, but only of light weapons. Jordanian artillery was now silent.

With me in the car were the chief of staff and the head of Central Command. We reached the arch of the Lions' Gate and entered the Old City together, side by side. This was indeed an historic moment.

In the very early hours of their first day of fighting, the paratroopers had suffered extremely heavy casualties; but on this morning, June 7, 1967, when they had broken into the Old City, no one had been hurt. The situation turned out to be as I had expected. After Jerusalem had been encircled and cut off from Jordan, the enemy troops who had remained laid down their weapons.

Photo on previous page: Moshe Dayan (center) and other top Israeli military officials walk in the Old City of Jerusalem for the first time in June 7, 1967. (© **AP Images.**)

Honoring a Sacred Spot

From the Lions' Gate we turned left and reached the Temple Mount. On the spire of the [Islamic] Dome of the Rock an Israeli flag fluttered. I ordered it to be taken down at once. If there was one thing we should refrain from doing in Jerusalem, it was putting flags on top of the mosque and the [Christian] Church of the Holy Sepulcher. We walked the length of the mount, then turned right through the Mograbi Gate and went down to the Western ("Wailing") Wall. The narrow plaza in front of the Wall was crowded with soldiers who had taken part in the grim battle for the liberation of Jerusalem. All were greatly moved, some wept openly, many prayed, all stretched out their hands to touch the hallowed stones.

I stood in silence facing the Wall.

I stood in silence facing the Wall. Then I took a small notebook out of my pocket, wrote a few words, and, following the Jewish tradition of centuries when pilgrims would press their written pleas and prayers in the crevices of the Wall, I folded the note and thrust it in an opening between the ashlars [stonework]. Moshe Pearlman, my special assistant, was somewhat surprised and asked what I had written. Without speaking I wrote again: "May peace descend upon the whole House of Israel."

When we left the Temple Mount area, a microphone was put in front of me for a few words on this historic occasion. I said: "We have returned to the holiest of our sites, and will never again be separated from it. To our Arab neighbors, Israel extends the hand of peace, and to the peoples of all faiths we guarantee full freedom of worship and of religious rights. We have come not to conquer the holy places of others, nor to diminish by the slightest measure their religious rights, but to ensure the unity of the city and to live in it with others in harmony."

On leaving the Western Wall, I had noticed some wild cyclamen of a delicate pinkish mauve sprouting between the Wall and the Mograbi Gate. I plucked a few to bring to Rahel [Dayan's wife]. I was sorry she could not have been there that day.

Though I had lived in Jerusalem for several years, I was not a Jerusalemite. Before 1948, when I had visited the Old City, it was as though I had stepped into another world, a world of thick stone walls that enclosed teeming bazaars crowded with shoppers and merchants, tourists and pilgrims from overseas, Arabs in their *kefiehs*, Hassidic Jews in their traditional black garb, and monks and nuns in the robes of their orders. Crooked steps led upward from the narrow market lanes and lost themselves in dark mysterious alleys. It was all very different from the Israel in which I was born and brought up, an Israel open and flooded with light. But now, on this day of its liberation, Jerusalem was unlike the city I had known. Paratroopers, tank-men, and troops of the Jerusalem Infantry Brigade filled the city, their weapons slung over their shoulders, exultation in their eyes. This was the Jerusalem we had yearned and fought for, this was our Jerusalem, Jewish Jerusalem, free and gay with celebration. But there was also sadness, sadness over the lives that had been lost in making this celebration possible, sadness at our first sight of the Jewish Quarter that had been destroyed in 1948.

Henceforth, it would again be the Jerusalem it had once been, the Jerusalem of all Israel.

On this day, Jerusalem belonged to the army that had liberated it. Henceforth, it would again be the Jerusalem it had once been, the Jerusalem of all Israel.

Opening the Gates to Peace

I ordered Uzi to open wide the gates in the Old City wall. We would need to consider and determine the arrangements for the now united city, west and east, and how to introduce a new harmonious pattern of living for the Jewish and Arab communities. This would take time. The walls of the Old City were a magnificent creation, with a grandeur more compelling than any monument in the world. But I did not want them to serve as a divisive barrier between the communities. I wanted their gates opened to the old and the new—in every sense.

I flew back to General Headquarters. Inside the helicopter I wrapped myself in my coat and curled up in a corner. Not that I wished to sleep, but I had no wish to talk. I was loath to dispel the feeling aroused by the vision of the liberated city. Jerusalem was closer to me than it had ever been. Never again would we be parted.

A Palestinian Child Becomes a Refugee

Amani Tayseer Kanaan

In the years since 1967, many Palestinian Arabs maintain they were unjustifiably uprooted by the conflict and, in effect, made homeless as the areas that they lived in passed from Jordanian to Israeli control. In the following viewpoint, Amani Tayseer Kanaan describes how her family was uprooted and how they continued to struggle after the Six-Day War was over. Kanaan was only seven years old during the war, but retains vivid memories of the short conflict as well as how, in later years, she and her family were subjects of an "occupying" power.

Some claim that there is a crucial incident, or turning point, in a person's past that serves as a thunderbolt and changes their lives forever. I was too young to clearly remember my thunderbolt. Yet, having witnessed

---

SOURCE. Amani Tayseer Kanaan, "The Occupation of Palestine Recollections," MUFTAH.org, September 15, 2011. Available at: http://muftah.org/the-occupation-of-palestine-childhood-recollections.

the Israeli occupation of Palestine in 1967, and the events that followed, I can safely say that mine started to roar and rumble at the tender age of seven.

> I viewed the Israeli soldiers as 'ogres.'

My recollections of that period are fuzzy, and unconnected. But I vividly remember that summer day of June 1967 when I was bundled into my father's car with my four-year-old sister, and three-year-old brother who was suffering from the mumps at the time and had to be constantly consoled. Together with our neighbours, we headed to Ramallah, a town 20 km outside of Jerusalem that my father had decided was safer than our neighbourhood in Jerusalem. We drove to a hotel owned by my parent's friend, where we were met by my two aunts and their families. We stayed there for one week, which was the duration of the war. I do not remember much about that period, except the tense atmosphere among the adults, and their constant reassurance to us kids that everything was going to be all right. Somehow, I knew that was not to be the case.

Having grown up in Jerusalem, where the other half of the city was occupied by Israel, I viewed the Israeli soldiers as "ogres" and always feared that they would one day cross the no-man's land into my beloved homeland. I had constant images of men with tails, and horns, invading our land, and taking over our lives. Now those deformed beings were here, and all we could do was wait for the inevitable.

The Radio blasted all day about Arab victories, and gradually I could see some hope returning, while preparations were made to go back home. On the seventh day of our confinement, I awoke to strange voices coming from the lobby. Upon investigating, I found all the adults assembled in the lobby with soldiers everywhere. Since there were no tails or horns in sight, I assumed that the Arab soldiers had finally come to save us.

My father was speaking in English in a quiet and tough tone, and the soldiers were standing around, some translating what my Dad was saying to others in a language that I'd never heard before. Looking around at the sombre faces, it suddenly struck me that those morning intruders were none other than our most dreaded enemy, Israeli soldiers.

They had arrived, and the nightmare was just beginning.

My Occupied Homeland

As I left the house on a shopping trip with my mother, the light drizzling rain turned into a steady downpour. I could not see clearly where I was going. I stopped to ask for directions from a young man taking cover under a bus stop kiosk. I was speaking in English, since we were in the Israeli sector of Jerusalem. He stared at me for a while, and then asked if I was an Arab. When I confirmed his suspicion, he spat in my face.

He stared at me for a while, and then asked if I was an Arab. When I confirmed his suspicion, he spat in my face.

That was in 1976 in Jerusalem where I was born. I was sixteen-years-old, full of dreams and romantic beliefs that I could and will change the world. To this day, this incident remains entrenched in my mind. I can still see that man running in the rain, while I was chasing after him (God only knows what I was planning to do if, or when, I caught up with him). My mother was chasing after me, horrified about what would happen if I actually caught him. Looking back now, I did not think of the fact that he could have hurt me and that no one would have attempted to stop him because he was from the privileged race, and I was a mere Arab. I still remember going back home drenched from the rain and my tears. I will never forget the utter humiliation and helplessness I felt at that moment, and continued to feel for many years after.

I don't really know when I started to have those feelings of great injustice, and extreme humiliation. Growing up in Jerusalem, I had an almost normal childhood, with all the joys, sadness, and contradictions which that period entails. But there was always the shadow of occupation that loomed overhead.

Before the onset of the war, my father was the chief Judge in Jerusalem's court. To this day, my regret is that I never witnessed my Dad at work in court, never saw him preside over a session, and never attended any of his court matters. It was not a choice that I made, I was obviously too young then to be involved in any of those activities. After the occupation, my father was faced with the choice of working with the Israelis, since courts in Jerusalem were placed under the occupier's jurisdiction, or refraining from any collaboration and going on strike. Obviously, he chose the latter.

Despite the limited sense of awareness that accompanies childhood, I was acutely aware of the constant tensions and frustrations that marked the period immediately following the occupation. It must have been devastating for my father who was still in his early forties to lose his job, as well as his homeland overnight. I started repeating the word depression, without knowing what it meant. My dad started developing lumps, mostly in the neck area because of all the tension, stress, and obsessive worrying that he was experiencing. With each new lump and the tests for possible malignancy that followed, our home turned into a ticking time bomb waiting to explode. Thankfully, with each test my father's lumps turned out to be benign, and we could breathe easily until the next one appeared.

Political Meetings Gained Very Little Ground

Visitors to our home were constant; some were familiar family friends and relatives, while others were complete

Palestinians flee Israel for Jordan, crossing over what remains of the Allenby Bridge on June 17, 1967. (© Bettmann/Corbis.)

strangers to me. Because of my dad's prominent position in the community, many political meetings took place in our house regarding the catastrophe that had befallen our nation and deciding how to deal with the new status quo. I was always hovering in the background trying to hear and understand what was going on. At that time, everybody believed it was still a reversible situation, and that Israel would eventually adhere to UN Resolution 242, which required Israel to return to the pre-1967 borders. Meetings were held with various foreign dignitaries to try pressuring their respective governments to convince Israel to withdraw. Demonstrations and protests were scheduled almost daily and civil disobedience actions were put into effect. Little did anyone know that all was futile and the Occupation was a "fait accompli" [a done deal] that would exist, and grow stronger with each passing year.

During the first few years of the Occupation, all Palestinian personalities, in the West Bank and Jerusalem, were adamant in their refusal to meet with any Israeli representing the Israeli government. They still believed that the occupation was a temporary situation that would eventually cease to exist. As the years dragged on, it became painfully obvious that this optimism was unrealistic, and that the existing situation would not change. On the contrary, each day brought newfound realities that made it difficult to even envision a foreseeable end to the disastrous facts on the ground.

After much debate, and consultations, it was decided that group and individual meetings would be held with Israeli officials. In hindsight, I can't imagine what they thought, or hoped to accomplish. What could they say that wasn't already said by friend and foe alike? What could they add to hundreds of files, and tens of UN resolutions tossed into archives, already gathering dust?

I started preparing for some of those meetings by drawing big posters, and writing various slogans about

Palestine being our country, and how we would resist and fight until we got our homeland back. Visitors to our house were greeted with a huge poster that read "Get Out of my Home and Country" right at the garden gate, and similar ones all the way up to our reception rooms where we received our guests. My parents never objected to my behaviour. On the contrary, I was always called to meet the visitors, and encouraged to give them a piece of my mind. My father must have thought that exposing them to my verbal onslaught communicated to them the fact that Palestinians, adults and children alike, would not accept the Occupation as a fact of life.

With the courage of a child unthreatened by any consequence, it soon became my passion to write articles for magazines, protest the Occupation to various NGOs [non-governmental organizations] and send SOSs [distress signals] to foreign dignitaries. I was bursting with a passionate urge to participate in efforts to regain my homeland and with it my very existence. Even play time with neighbourhood friends evolved into staged wars for the liberation of Palestine. Most of the kids refused to play Israeli soldiers, so the war always reverted to Cowboys v. Indians, yet I would secretly pretend that the other team was made up of Israeli soldiers, and I was the long-awaited Palestinian hero come to take back what was rightfully mine. I would spend hours lecturing neighbourhood kids on our unenviable situation, parroting bits and pieces of what I had heard from my father and his friends.

My adolescent years continued in very much the same way, only with a change of venue and audience. Every project or report I did in school always somehow referred to the occupation, even if it was irrelevant to the given subject. It became a source of irritation for the German nuns who were my teachers. I was cautioned and scolded continuously, yet I never gave in. I was chosen as class speaker for the senior class, and although I was warned by the principal not to go into any "unsavoury subjects," I managed to turn the graduation ceremony into a political rally.

A Teenager Under Occupation

Unbelievable as it might appear, I was, until that point, living in a protected environment, where the truly ugly side of the Occupation was obscured and only evident to adults. It is true that it was a persistent part of my life, which I constantly heard about and that I knew had repercussions for the people around me, especially my father. However, the older I got the more evident the Occupation's ugliness became. The stark reality was becoming increasingly real. Being a young Palestinian adult meant being stopped at check points, being asked for IDs, and being subjected to all the humiliation of being treated as a foreigner in your own country on your land and that of your forefathers.

Palestine was the only place I could call home. It was the only Homeland I knew, and somewhere along the line, I had become a stranger, a refugee in my own land. The feeling of bitterness and overwhelming helplessness had become a constant companion. Several incidents at that time intensified my feelings of injustice. The epitome of humiliation was crossing the Allenby Bridge, which served as the border between Jordan and the West Bank. Security steps outshone any other procedure known to man! There were endless lines, while Israeli soldiers on duty intentionally took their time displaying for everybody underwear and other personal items they found in the suitcases they searched. They never neglected to make rude comments and ridicule us. As if that was not enough, they artfully scattered and threw everything around, making mounds of clothing, shoes, and other items. One always ended up with someone else's belongings, and in the process lost quite a few others.

To add insult to injury, shoes, which were apparently a "security hazard," were piled up in a heap, while we "worthless" Palestinians walked around barefoot and were checked, probed, and pushed around.

I will never forget the day I was coming back to Jerusalem after a brief visit to Jordan with my family. I had just gotten a new gold pendant for my sixteenth birthday, with the word Palestine carved on it. I was so proud wearing it, and I thought it looked amazing. Apparently the Israeli soldier interrogating me—"part of the procedure at the bridge"—did not share my sentiment.

> I had no homeland, and obviously, I was not even allowed to keep my Dignity.

He cruelly informed me that my pendant was to be confiscated, since no such thing as Palestine existed, and that wearing it presented a security breach to the "State of Israel." I adamantly refused. I was taken to the office of the chief military commander of the border, and was ordered to hand it over. After much pleading from my mother, I eventually threw it at them, and through my choking tears, told them that they could take Palestine off my neck, but never from my heart.

I had no homeland, and obviously, I was not even allowed to keep my Dignity.

Report on the Razing of Emmaus, Beit Nuba, and Yalou in 1967

Amos Kenan

In the following viewpoint, Amos Kenan recalls how, as a soldier in Israel's army reserve, he saw his unit participate in the destruction of three Arab villages during the Six-Day War on the grounds that those villages, located to the west of Jerusalem, were refuges for Arab fighters. Kenan writes how very little concern was shown for the civilian inhabitants of those villages, who were turned into refugees. He also notes how the opinions of his fellow soldiers toward the events varied greatly and expresses his belief that by turning peaceful villagers into refugees, Israel was creating future enemies. Kenan is considered one of the founders of modern Israeli culture and worked as a sculptor, film director, and newspaper columnist. He is the author of *With Whips and Scorpions* and *The Road to Ein Harod.*

SOURCE. Amos Kenan, "Report on the Razing of Emmaus, Beit Nuba, and Yalou in 1967," *Israel: A Wasted Victory*, 1970. www.PalestineRemembered.com.

Amos Kenan, a reservist Israeli soldier, took part in the fighting in this region. This report has been sent to all Knesseth Members. This English version is from Israel: A Wasted Victory, *Amikam Tel-Aviv Publishers Ltd., Tel-Aviv 1970, pp. 18–21.*

Beit Nuba village near Latrun,

The commander of my platoon said that it had been decided to blow up the three villages in the sector—Yalou, Beit Nuba and Amwas. For reasons of strategy, tactics, security. In the first place, to straighten out the Latrun "finger". Secondly, in order to punish these murderers' dens. And thirdly, to deprive infiltrators of a base in the future.

One may argue with this idiotic approach, which advocates collective punishment and is based on the belief that if the infiltrator loses one house, he will not find another from which to wait in ambush. One may argue with the effectiveness of increasing the number of our enemies—but why argue?

We were told it was our job to search the village houses; that if we found any armed men there, they were to be taken prisoner. Any unarmed persons should be given time to pack their belongings and then told to get moving—get moving to Beit Sira, a village not far away. We were also told to take up positions around the approaches to the villages, in order to prevent those villagers who had heard the Israeli assurances over the radio that they could return to their homes in peace—from returning to their homes. The order was—shoot over their heads and tell them there is no access to the village.

The homes in Beit Nuba are beautiful stone houses, some of them luxurious mansions. Each house stands in an orchard of olives, apricots and grapevines; there are also cypresses and other trees grown for their beauty and the shade they give. Each tree stands in its carefully watered bed. Between the trees, lie neatly hoed and weeded rows of vegetables.

In the houses we found a wounded Egyptian commando officer and some old men and women. At noon the first bulldozer arrived, and ploughed under the house closest to the village edge.

Amos Kenan saw firsthand the destruction of Arab villages by the Israeli army and believes their actions created not only refugees but future enemies. (© **Ulf Andersen/Getty Images.**)

With one sweep of the bulldozer, the cypresses and the olive-trees were uprooted. Ten more minutes pass and the house, with its meagre furnishings and belongings, has become a mass of rubble. After three houses had been mowed down, the first convoy of refugees arrives, from the direction of Ramallah. We did not shoot into the air. We did take up positions for coverage, and those of us who spoke Arabic went up to them to give them the orders. There were old men hardly able to walk, old women mumbling to themselves, babies in their mother's arms, small children, small children weeping, begging for water. The convoy waved white flags.

We told them to move on to Beit Sira. They said that wherever they went, they were driven away, that nowhere were they allowed to stay. They said they had been on the way for four days now—without food or water; some had perished on the way. They asked only to be allowed back into their own village; and said we would do better to kill them. Some had brought with them a goat, a sheep, a camel or a donkey. A father crunched grains of wheat in his hand to soften them so that his four children might have something to eat. On the horizon, we spotted the next line approaching. One man was carrying a 50-kilogram sack of flour on his back, and that was how he had walked mile after mile. More old men, more women, more babies. They flopped down exhausted at the spot where they were told to sit. Some had brought along a cow or two, or a calf—all their earthly possessions. We did not allow them to go into the village to pick up their belongings, for the order was that they must not be allowed to see their homes being destroyed. The children wept, and some of the soldiers wept too. We went to look for water but found none. We stopped an army vehicle in which sat a Lieutenant-Colonel, two

We did not allow them to go into the village . . . [for] they must not be allowed to see their homes being destroyed.

captains and a woman. We took a jerry-can of water from them and tried to make it go round among the refugees. We handed out sweets and cigarettes. More of our soldiers wept. We asked the officers why the refugees were being sent back and forth and driven away from everywhere they went. The officers said it would do them good to walk and asked "why worry about them, they're only Arabs"? We were glad to learn that half-an-hour later, they were all arrested by the military police, who found their car stacked with loot. More and more lines of refugees kept arriving. By this time there must have been hundreds of them. They couldn't understand why they had been told to return, and now were not being allowed to return. One could not remain unmoved by their entreaties. Someone asked what was the point of destroying the houses—why didn't the Israelis go live in them instead? The platoon commander decided to go to headquarters to find out whether there was any written order as to what should be done with them, where to send them and to try and arrange transportation for the women and children, and food supplies. He came back and said there was no written order; we were to drive them away.

Like lost sheep they went on wandering along the roads. The exhausted were rescued. Towards evening we learned that we had been told a falsehood—at Beit Sira too, the bulldozers had begun their work of destruction, and the refugees had not been allowed to enter. We also learned that it was not in our sector alone that areas were being "straightened out"; the same was going on in all sectors. Our word had not been a word of honor; the policy was a policy without backing.

The soldiers grumbled. The villagers clenched their teeth as they watched the bulldozer mow down trees. At night we stayed on to guard the bulldozers, but the entire battalion was seething with anger; most of them did not want to do the job. In the morning we were transferred to another spot. No one could understand how Jews could do such a thing. Even those who justified the action said that it should have been possible to provide shelter for the population; that a final decision should have been taken as to their fate as to where they were to go. The refugees should have been taken to their new home, together with their property. No one could understand why the fellah should be barred from taking his oil-stove, his blanket and some provisions.

The chickens and the pigeons were buried under the rubble. The fields were turned to desolation before our eyes, and the children who dragged themselves along the road that day, weeping bitterly, will be the *fedayeen* of 19 years hence.

That is how that day, we lost the victory.

The CIA Analyzes the Six-Day War

David S. Robarge

The following selection was written by David S. Robarge, a member of the CIA's history staff. Robarge discusses the role of then director of central intelligence Richard Helms as he navigated the CIA through the 1967 Arab-Israeli War. The analysis of the intelligence gathered by the CIA about the 1967 war was accurate and had an immediate impact on US foreign policy. Their performance during the crisis ultimately redeemed the CIA in the eyes of US president Lyndon B. Johnson.

With all the attention paid of late to intelligence failures, it is easy to forget that sometimes the intelligence process has worked almost perfectly. On those occasions, most of the right information was collected in a timely fashion, analyzed with appropriate methodologies, and punctually disseminated

SOURCE. David S. Robarge, "CIA Analysis of 1967 Arab-Israeli War," CIA.gov, April 15, 2007. Reproduced courtesy of Central Intelligence Agency.

in finished form to policymakers who were willing to read and heed it. Throughout those situations, the intelligence bureaucracies were responsive and cooperative, and the Director of Central Intelligence had access and influence downtown. One such example that can be publicly acknowledged arose in 1967 in a familiar flash point area—the Middle East—and put Director of Central Intelligence (DCI) Richard Helms in the position of making or breaking his, and the CIA's, reputation with one of the most difficult and demanding presidents the United States has ever had—Lyndon Johnson.

In his memoir, Helms wrote that:

> Russell Jack Smith, former director for intelligence [analysis at the CIA], has described my working relationship with President Johnson as "golden"—in the sense that it was close to the maximum that any DCI might hope to achieve. However comforting, this assessment is too generous. It was not my relationship with LBJ [Lyndon Johnson] that mattered, it was his perception of the value of the data and the assessments the Agency was providing him that carried the day.

Certainly the key intelligence achievement that "carried the day" for Helms and the CIA under Johnson was the Agency's strikingly accurate analysis about the Arab-Israeli war of June 1967. It was one of those rare instances when unpoliticized intelligence had a specific, clear-cut, and immediate impact on US foreign policy. The CIA was right about the timing, duration, and outcome of the war; the judgments quickly reached US leaders in an immediately usable form; and the Agency did not temper its analysis when faced with policymaker resistance. The whole 1967 war intelligence scenario demonstrated that well-substantiated findings advocated by a respected DCI with access to the White House could win out over political pressures and policymakers' predilections.

Relations with the White House

It was especially important for Helms and the CIA to impress Lyndon Johnson because he had little experience with or interest in intelligence when he suddenly became president in November 1963, and his attitudes had not changed appreciably during his early years in office. Johnson's selection of the hapless William Raborn to replace the strong-willed John McCone as Agency director in April 1965 clearly indicated where he placed the CIA in the power structure of his administration. He preferred getting "VIP gossip" from FBI Director J. Edgar Hoover instead of facts and analysis from the CIA. At the time he appointed Helms as DCI in June 1966, LBJ was not yet convinced that intelligence could advance his policies, and he already was annoyed at the Agency's negativism about Vietnam. In addition, after the public scandal in early 1967 over the CIA's funding of political covert action programs—the so-called Ramparts revelations—Helms was anxious to redeem the CIA with the president.

Johnson was a hard sell, however, and a harder mind to penetrate. Helms's director for analysis, R. Jack Smith, has told of his own frustration over a White House assignment to evaluate the pros and cons of a new US initiative in Vietnam that involved substantially stepping up the war effort:

> If one based one's decision on the conclusions of our study, the result was obvious: the gain was not worth the cost. Nevertheless, the President announced the next day that he intended to go ahead. Distinctly annoyed that an admirable piece of analysis, done under forced draft at White House request, was being ignored, I stomped into Helms's office. "How in the hell can the President make that decision in the face of our findings?" I asked.
>
> Dick fixed me with a sulphurous look. "How do I know how he made up his mind? How does any president make decisions? Maybe Lynda Bird was in favor of

> it. Maybe one of his old friends urged him. Maybe it was something he read. Don't ask me to explain the workings of a president's mind."

The period before and during the 1967 war gave Helms an opportunity to act on two of the several elements of his intelligence credo, which he often expressed in catch phrases: "You only work for one president at a time" and "Stay at the table." Helms well understood that each president has his own appreciation of intelligence and his own way of dealing with the CIA. A director who does not learn to live with those peculiarities will soon render himself irrelevant. Helms also knew that a CIA director must remember that he runs a service organization whose products must be timely and cogent to be of value to the First Consumer. Because Helms was keenly attuned to Johnson's take on the CIA and already had its analytical apparatus in "task force mode" by May 1967, the Agency could immediately respond to White House questions about the looming crisis in Arab-Israeli relations.

The Middle East Heats Up

On the morning of 23 May—the day after Egypt closed the Gulf of Aqaba, Israel's only access to the Red Sea—President Johnson summoned Helms from a congressional briefing and tasked him with providing an assessment of the increasingly volatile Middle East situation. Here was a chance for the CIA to seize the day analytically. Only four hours later—just in time for one of LBJ's "Tuesday lunches"—Helms had in hand two papers: "US Knowledge of Egyptian Alert" and "Overall Arab and Israeli Military Capabilities." Those memoranda, plus a Situation Report (SITREP), were delivered to him in the ground floor lobby outside the White House office of presidential adviser Walt Rostow. The remarkably rapid turnaround was possible because the Directorate of Intelligence's (DI) Arab-Israeli task force, in existence since early in the year, already was producing two SITREPs a day, and the Office of Current Intelligence (OCI) had for months been keeping a running log of the two sides' relative strengths and states of readiness. The second paper Helms had brought—the "who will win" memo—was the crucial one. It stated that Israel could "defend successfully against simultaneous Arab attacks on all fronts . . . or hold on any three fronts while mounting successfully a major offensive on the fourth."

Two days later, Tel Aviv [the Israeli government] muddled this clear intelligence picture by submitting to Washington a Mossad estimate that claimed the Israeli military was badly outgunned by a Soviet-backed Arab war machine. The Israelis may have been trying to exploit the special relationship they had with James Angleton, chief of CIA counterintelligence. For years, Angleton had run the Israeli account out of his Counterintelligence Staff, without involving the Directorate of Plans's Near East Division. That unusual arrangement may have given Tel Aviv a sense that Washington accorded its analyses such special import that US leaders would listen to its judgments on Arab-Israeli issues over those of their own intelligence services.

Helms had the Office of National Estimates (ONE) prepare an appraisal of the Mossad assessment, which was ready in only five hours. ONE flatly stated: "We do not believe that the Israeli appreciation . . . was a serious estimate of the sort they would submit to their own high officials." Rather, "it is probably a gambit intended to influence the US to . . . provide military supplies . . . make more public commitments to Israel . . . approve Israeli military initiatives, and . . . put more pressure on [Egyptian president Gamal Abdel] Nasser." ONE further concluded—contrary to Tel Aviv's suspicions—that "the Soviet aim is still to avoid military involvement and to give the US a black eye among the Arabs by identifying it with Israel"; Moscow "probably could not openly help the Arabs because of lack of capability, and probably would not for fear of confrontation with the US." It was this latter ONE judgment that caused [secretary of state] Dean Rusk to remark to Helms, "if this is a mistake, it's a beaut." The same judgment triggered an order from the president to Helms and Joint Chiefs of Staff Chairman Earle Wheeler to "scrub it down." Helms returned to CIA headquarters and told the Board of National Estimates to produce a coordinated assessment by the next day.

Making the Right Call

That paper—issued the following afternoon with the title "Military Capabilities of Israel and the Arab States"—is the illustrious "special estimate" in which the CIA (in collaboration with the Defense Intelligence Agency) purportedly called the war right, from its outcome down to the day it would end. It actually was a memorandum, not a Special National Intelligence Estimate, and although drafts had said that the Israelis would need seven to nine days to reach the Suez Canal, that precision was sacrificed in the coordination process. Instead, the paper estimated that Israeli armored forces could breach Egypt's forward lines in the Sinai within "several" days. In another memorandum issued the same day, ONE doubted that Moscow had encouraged the Egyptian president's provocations and concluded that it would not intervene with its own forces to save the Arabs from defeat. As one senior Agency analyst who helped write these papers later remarked: "Rarely has the Intelligence Community spoken as clearly, as rapidly, and with such unanimity."

Informed by these assessments, President Johnson declined to airlift special military supplies to Israel or even to publicly support it. He later recalled bluntly telling Israeli Foreign Minister Abba Eban, "All of our intelligence people are unanimous that if the UAR [United Arab Republic] attacks, you will whip hell out of them."

Having answered one crucial question of the president's—how would the war end?—Helms also was able to warn him when it was about to begin. According to several published accounts, Helms met on 1 June with a senior Israeli official who hinted that Israel could no longer avoid a decision. Its restraint thus far was due to American pressure, but, he said, the delay had cost Israel the advantage of surprise. Helms interpreted the remarks as suggesting that Israel would attack very soon. Moreover, according to Helms, the official stated clearly that although Israel expected US diplomatic backing and the delivery of weapons already agreed upon, it would request no additional support and did not expect any. The official abruptly left the United States on 2 June along with the Israeli ambassador. That morning, according to published accounts, Helms wrote an "Eyes Only" letter to President Johnson, forewarning that Israel probably would start a war within a few days.

Israel Launches Its Attack

Helms was awakened at 3:00 in the morning on 5 June by a call from the CIA Operations Center. The Foreign Broadcast Information Service had picked up reports that Israel had launched its attack. (OCI soon concluded that the Israelis—contrary to their claims—had fired first.) President Johnson was gratified that because of CIA analyses and Helms's tip, he could inform congressional leaders later in the day that he had been expecting Israel's move.

During the brief war, Helms went to the White House every day but one, reporting to the NSC [National Security Council] and the president's special committee of Middle East experts, using the outpouring of SITREPs from OCI (five a day), DI special memoranda, the *President's Daily Brief*, and other analytical products. "In the midst of one meeting," Helms recalled,

> LBJ suddenly fixed his attention on me in my usual seat at the end of the long table. "Dick," he snapped, "just how accurate is your intelligence on the progress of this war?" Without having a moment to consider the evidence, I shot from the hip, "It's accurate just as long as the Israelis are winning." It may have sounded as if I were smarting off, but it was the exact truth, and it silenced [those around] the table. Only an amused twitch of [former secretary of state and Johnson adviser] Dean Acheson's mustache suggested his having noted my reasoning.

The Soviet Union Weighs In

On 10 June, as Israeli victory appeared near, the White House received a message over the "Hot Line" from Soviet premier Alexei Kosygin. The Kremlin foresaw a "grave catastrophe" and threatened to take "necessary actions . . . including military" if the Israelis did not halt their advance across the Golan Heights. Helms was in the Situation Room with several other presidential advisers when the message from the Kremlin came over from the Pentagon, where the Hot Line teletype was located. Helms remembered the setting as "unlike the Hollywood versions of situation rooms . . . there were no flashing lights, no elaborate projections of maps and photographs on a silver screen, or even any armed guards rigidly at attention beside the doorway. The room itself was painted a bleak beige and furnished simply with an oval conference table and an assortment of comfortable chairs."

Helms recalled the hush and chill that fell over the room after the translation of Kosygin's message was checked. "The room went silent as abruptly as if a radio had been switched off. . . . The conversation was conducted in the lowest voices I have ever heard. . . . It seemed impossible to believe that five years after the missile confrontation in Cuba, the two superpowers had again squared off." On the recommendation of Secretary of Defense Robert McNamara (endorsed by all present), Johnson dispatched the Sixth Fleet to the eastern Mediterranean—a move intended to convey American resolve without backing the Soviets into a corner. Helms told the president that Russian submarines monitoring the fleet's movement would immediately report that it had changed course. Moscow got the message, and a cease-fire later that day restored an uneasy peace to the region.

Putting Together the Intelligence Package

Altogether, as Helms put it, "we had presented the boss with a tidy package." Several circumstances made this success possible:

- Policymakers asked one clear, basic question: Who will win if the US stays out? Analysts did not have to advance vague medium- or long-term predictions that could go wrong because of unforeseen or high impact/low probability events.
- Analysts had hard data—military statistics and reliable information on weapons systems—to work with, not just "tea leaves" to read. This episode was not a Middle East version of Kremlinology.
- The evidence was on the CIA's side. Israel could not prove its case that the Arab armies would trounce it.
- The crisis was brief. The time span between the reporting of warning indicators and the playing out of key analytical judgments was around three weeks. There was not enough time for the basic issues to become fogged over.

The CIA Gains the President's Trust

The CIA's analytical achievement brought short-term political benefits for Helms and the Agency. From then on, Johnson included Helms in all Tuesday lunches—the director had attended them occasionally since his appointment in 1966, but after the 1967 war he was assured of what he later called "the hottest ticket in town." It was at these inner sanctum discussions that Helms fulfilled what he regarded as perhaps his greatest responsibility as DCI: seeing that he "kept the game honest"—presenting just the facts and analyses based on them, and staying out of policy discussions. "Without objectivity," Helms said in a 1971 speech, "there is no credibility, and an intelligence organization without credibility is of little use to those it serves." Johnson appreciated that tough edge to Helms's style, and their good professional rapport helped alleviate some of the tension that the Agency's discordant analyses on Vietnam were causing.

A few years after leaving the CIA, Helms said of the Agency's analysis of the 1967 war: "When you come as close as that in the intelligence business, it has to be regarded pretty much as a triumph." The CIA's timely and accurate intelligence before and during the war had won Helms, literally and figuratively, a place at the president's table—perhaps the most precious commodity that a DCI could possess. It also is one of the most perishable—a painful lesson that several directors since Helms have had to relearn, to their, and the Agency's, detriment.

CHRONOLOGY

1897	The First Zionist Congress takes place in Basel, Switzerland. It represents the move by activist European Jews to create a modern Jewish state in Palestine by establishing settlements alongside the population of Jews already living there.
1917	In the Balfour Declaration, Great Britain, which is to take possession of Palestine after World War I (1914–1918), promises to support the creation of a Jewish state while at the same time recognizing the rights of Palestinian Arabs.
1929	Violent riots erupt in Jerusalem, resulting in the deaths of 133 Jews mostly at the hands of Arabs and 116 Arabs mostly at the hands of British authorities.
1936–1939	An Arab revolt in Palestine, inspired by an escalation in the arrival of Jews from Nazi-dominated Europe, results in the deaths of more than five thousand people.
1937	The British Peel Commission proposes the creation of separate Jewish and Palestinian states. It is the first of several such moves.
1939–1945	During World War II, Nazi Germany massacres some six million European Jews in the Holocaust.
1947	February: Great Britain announces it is turning Palestine over to the United Nations.

November 29: The United Nations approves a plan to partition Palestine into two states. While Jewish leaders approve it, Arabs reject the plan.

May 14: Israel declares its national independence.

May 15: The First Arab-Israeli War begins as Egypt, Syria, Lebanon, Iraq, Jordan, and Arab militant groups try to destroy Israel.

1949 Over several months, Israel enters into peace agreements with Arab states, ending the war and dividing former British Palestine among Israel, Jordan, and Egypt. Along the way some one hundred thousand Palestinian Arabs become refugees.

1956 During the Suez Crisis, Israeli, British, and French forces invade Egyptian territory along the Sinai Peninsula to prevent Egypt from establishing complete control of the Suez Canal. The effort is largely a failure, strengthening the hand of Egyptian president Gamal Abdel Nasser. The United Nations sends an emergency force (UNEF) to maintain order in Sinai.

1961 Egypt and Syria create the United Arab Republic (UAR) as a symbol of Pan-Arabism, or Arab unity. Nasser is its first president. Syria withdraws from the union in 1961 though Nasser remains focused on Pan-Arabism and refers to Egypt and a loose network of allies as the UAR.

1964 The Palestine Liberation Organization (PLO) is created in Cairo, Egypt.

1967 May: Reports from the Soviet Union, later proven to be false, lead Egypt and Syria to think that Israel plans an invasion of Syria. Both nations begin to prepare for war.

May 15: In response to the Egyptian military buildup in Sinai, Israel prepares its defenses while trying to assure Egypt it has no aggressive intentions.

May 16: President Nasser demands the withdrawal of the UNEF from Sinai. UN secretary general U Thant agrees to do so a day later.

May 23: Egypt closes the Straits of Tiran to Israeli shipping, an act generally understood to be an act of war under international law.

June 5: The Six-Day War begins as Israel launches a surprise attack, targeting a massive Egyptian military buildup in Sinai. The surprise attack results in the destruction of much of the Egyptian Air Force. Syria and Jordan launch attacks on Israel.

June 6: Israeli forces take control of the Gaza Strip. Jordanian troops are ordered to withdraw from the West Bank.

June 7: Israeli troops take East Jerusalem, formerly in Jordanian hands.

June 8: Facing continued defeats in Sinai, Egypt accepts a ceasefire called for by the United Nations.

Israeli aircraft and gunboats attack the USS *Liberty*, a US naval vessel, off the coast of Egypt. Enquiries later determine the attack was an unfortunate mistake.

June 9: Israel and Syria continue fighting with a focus on the Golan Heights.

June 10: Syria and Israel agree on a ceasefire, bringing the Six-Day War to an end. Some 750,000 Palestinian Arabs become refugees.

September 17: Meeting in Khartoum, Sudan, Arab leaders conclude what comes to be known as the "3 no's": no to peace with Israel, no to diplomatic recognition of Israel, and no to negotiation with Israel.

November 22: The United Nations passes Resolution 242. It calls for Israel to withdraw from the territories it occupied in the Six-Day War and for further negotiations.

1969–1970 The Palestine Liberation Organization fights a war of attrition against Israel, consisting of terrorist attacks and retaliations.

1973 October: The Yom Kippur War pits Israel against Egypt, Syria, Jordan, Iraq, and Lebanon. The result is another Israeli victory, although Arab armies fight well.

1978 Egypt and Israel conclude the Camp David Accords in which Egypt becomes the first Arab state to grant Israel official recognition while Israel agrees to return the Sinai Peninsula to Egypt.

1982 Israel completes the pullout of its forces from Sinai.

1987 The first intifada (uprising) begins among Palestinian Arabs. It consists of demonstrations, boycotts, and some violent attacks against Israel, which responds in kind.

1988 Palestinian leaders declare national independence, although no actual state exists.

1993 Israel and the PLO conclude the Oslo Accords, in which the PLO agrees to recognize Israel's right to exist, and Israel grants Palestinian rule to Gaza and the city of Jericho in the West Bank.

1994 Israel and Jordan conclude a broad peace treaty solidifying diplomatic relations.

2000 A second intifada begins, lasting until 2005.

2011 US president Barack Obama urges the creation of a Palestinian state based on the borders that existed before the Six-Day War.

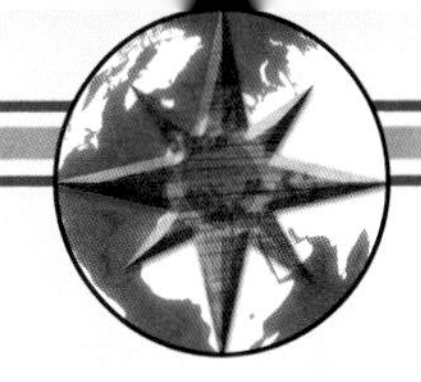

FOR FURTHER READING

Books

Anne Alexander, *Nasser: Life and Times.* London: Haus Publishing, 2005.

Jeremy Bowen, *Six Days: How the 1967 War Shaped the Middle East.* London: Simon & Schuster, 2003.

L.A. Brand, *Palestinians in the Arab World.* New York: Columbia University Press, 1988.

Randolph S. Churchill and Winston S. Churchill, *The Six Day War.* London: Heinemann Press, 1967.

Gregory Harms, *The Palestine-Israel Conflict: An Introduction.* London: Pluto Press, 2008.

Chaim Herzog, *The Arab-Israeli Wars: War and Peace in the Middle East.* New York: Vintage Books, 2005.

Albert Hourani, *The Emergence of the Modern Middle East.* London: Macmillan, 1981.

Walter Laqueur and Barry Rubin, eds., *The Arab-Israeli Reader,* revised ed. New York: Penguin, 2008.

William Roger Lewis and Avi Shlaim, eds., *The 1967 Arab-Israeli War: Origins and Consequences.* New York: Cambridge University Press, 2012.

Michael B. Oren, *Six Days of War: June 1967 and the Making of the Modern Middle East.* New York: Presidio Press, 2003.

Ilan Pappe, *The Israel/Palestine Question.* London: Routledge, 1999.

Richard B. Parker, *The Six Day War: A Retrospective.* Gainesville: University of Florida Press, 1996.

William B. Quandt, *Peace Process: American Diplomacy and the Arab-Israeli Conflict Since 1967.* Berkeley: Brookings Institution and the University of California Press, 2005.

Tom Segev, *1967: Israel, the War, and the Year that Transformed the Middle East*. New York: Metropolitan Books, 2007.

Periodicals and Internet Souces

Fouad Ajami, "The End of Pan-Arabism," *Foreign Affairs*, Winter 1978–1979.

Laura James, "Nasser and His Enemies: Foreign Policy Decision-Making in Egypt on the Eve of the Six Day War," *Middle East Review of International Affairs*, vol. 9, no. 2, 2005.

Rory McCarthy, "Ahmad Shalabi, 51, a Palestinian Refugee in Jordan," *The Guardian*, June 4, 2007.

Helen Schary Motro, "Six Day War: Fearing the Worst in '67," *Milwaukee Journal Sentinel*, June 3, 2007.

Dan Murphy, "What's So 'Shocking' About Obama Mentioning 1967 Borders?," *Christian Science Monitor*, May 20, 2011.

Michael B. Oren, "Did Israel Want the Six Day War?," *Azure*, no. 7, Spring 1999.

Ephraim Sneh, "Bad Borders, Good Neighbors," *New York Times*, July 10, 2011.

Time, "Middle East: The Quickest War," June 16, 1967.

Sandy Tolan, "Rethinking Israel's David-and-Goliath Past," *Salon*, June 4, 2007.

Conal Urquardt, "Six Days in June," *Observer*, May 5, 2007.

Conal Urquardt, Nidaa Hassan, and Martin Chulov, "Israeli Troops Clash on Syrian Border with Protesters Marking Six-Day War," *Guardian*, June 5, 2011.

Washington Report on Middle East Affairs, "Life in Gaza Before—and After—the 1967 War," May–June 2007.

Websites

Defensible Borders for a Lasting Peace (www.defensibleborders.org). This website provides historical material, news articles, and other resources that support the argument that Israel must keep some of the territories it gained in 1967 for the sake of national security.

Israel and Palestine: A Brief History (www.mideastweb.org/briefhistory.htm). Part of a larger website covering the Middle East, this page provides a history of the relationship between Israel and Palestine as well as links to books, articles, and other resources.

Six Day War (www.sixdaywar.co.uk). This website is a comprehensive resource on the Six-Day War with a largely pro-Israel viewpoint. It contains timelines, personal accounts, movie clips, and links to historical documents and articles on the conflict.

United Nations Relief and Works Agency for Palestine Refugees (www.unrwa.org). Providing interviews, film clips, news articles, and other materials, this website is maintained by an organization connected with the United Nations that acts on behalf of some 5 million Palestinian refugees in Syria, Jordan, Lebanon, and Israel.

INDEX

T